Braun and Schneider

HISTORIC
COSTUME
IN PICTURES

Dover Publications, Inc., New York

Published in Canada by General Publishing Company, Ltd., 30 Lesmill Road, Don Mills, Toronto, Ontario.
Published in the United Kingdom by Constable and Company, Ltd., 10 Orange Street, London, WC2.

This Dover edition, first published in 1975, contains all the plates from the third edition of *Costumes of All Nations*, as published by H. Grevel and Co., London, in 1907. Plates 124 and 125 have been supplied from a copy of the German publication on which the British was based, *Zur Geschichte der Kostüme*, as published by Braun & Schneider, Munich, n.d. The plates were originally published serially by Braun & Schneider between 1861 and 1890. The original artwork used for reproduction was in color.

The Publisher's Note, table of contents and captions have been prepared specially for the present edition, in which the sequence of plates has been altered. The text of the original German and British editions has not been used.

International Standard Book Number: 0-486-23150-X
Library of Congress Catalog Card Number: 74-12532

Manufactured in the United States of America
Dover Publications, Inc.
180 Varick Street
New York, N.Y. 10014

Publisher's Note

THE 125 LARGE COSTUME PLATES reprinted were originally issued periodically by the publishers Braun & Schneider in Munich between 1861 and 1890 (Plates 117 and 122 of the present edition are dated 1880; Plate 119, 1886).

When collected in bound volumes (which appeared in several editions in Germany and England from 1874 to the turn of the century), the plates were kept in the meaningless sequence in which they had first been issued. This sequence has been replaced here by chronological order.

Even in the old British editions the captions remained in German. They have been translated fully here for the first time (with modern place names given wherever possible), and a new table of contents replaces its cumbersome equivalent in the early editions.

Some of the early editions were in color, with the color varying somewhat fancifully from one edition to another. It seemed best to reissue this work in black and white.

The credits to artists found on the original plates are as follows (the plate numbers are those of the present edition):

M. Adamo: Plate 90.

L. Braun: Plate 89.

H. Engl: Plate 104.

J. Gehrts: Plate 6.

Carl Häberlin: Plates 20, 21, 26, 28, 30, 31, 39, 40, 41, 42, 43, 46, 47, 48, 49, 57, 58, 59, 60, 61, 63, 64, 65, 72, 73, 74, 75, 77, 78, 80, 81, 91, 96, 99, 101, 105, 106, 107, 108, 111, 112, 113, 114, 115, 116, 118, 119, 120, 124, 125.

Andreas Müller: Plates 1, 2, 3, 4, 5, 7, 8, 12, 14, 50, 67, 84.

F. Rothbart: Plate 23.

H. Schneider: Plate 45.

F. Simm: Plates 76 & 88.

J. Watter: Plates 86 & 92.

K. Weigand: Plate 32.

List of Plates

(1) Ancient Near East

(2) Ancient Near East

(3) Ancient Greece

(4) Ancient Rome

(5) Ancient Judaea

(6) Ancient Germans

(7) 4th to 6th Centuries

(8) Byzantine Empire

(9) 6th Century; Byzantine Empire

(10) 5th to 10th Centuries (and Ancient Egypt)

(11) 700–800; Carolingians

(12) 10th Century

(13) 11th Century

(14) 12th Century

(15) 13th Century

(16) 12th & 13th Centuries; Military-Religious Orders

(17) 14th Century

(18) 14th Century

(19) 14th Century; England

(20) 14th Century; Germany

(21) Second Half of the 14th Century; Italy

(22) First Half of the 15th Century

(23) First Half of the 15th Century

(24) Second Half of the 15th Century

(25) 15th Century; Italy

(26) 15th Century; France

(27) 15th Century; France and England

(28) Mid-15th Century; Burgundy

(29) Second Half of the 15th Century; Burgundy and Holland

(30) 15th Century; Germany

(31) 15th Century; Swiss Military Costume

(32) 15th and 16th Centuries

(33) First Third of the 16th Century

(34) Second Third of the 16th Century

(35) Last Third of the 16th Century

(36) First Third of the 16th Century; Germany

(37) First Third of the 16th Century; Germany

(38) First Third of the 16th Century; Germany

(39) First Third of the 16th Century; German Military Costume

(40) Mid-16th Century; Germany

(41) Late 16th Century; Germany

(42) Late 16th Century; Frisia

(43) 16th Century; France

(44) 16th Century; Poland and Russia

(45) 16th Century; Italy

(46) Late 16th Century (1583); Italy

(47) 16th Century; England

(48) 16th and 17th Centuries; England

(49) 16th and 17th Centuries

(50) 16th and 17th Centuries; Ecclesiastical Vestments

(51) First Half of the 17th Century

(52) Second Third of the 17th Century

(53) Second Third of the 17th Century

(54) Last Third of the 17th Century

(55) 17th Century; England

(56) First Third of the 17th Century; Netherlands

(57) First Third of the 17th Century; Germany

(58) Mid-17th Century; German Lands

(59) First Third of the 17th Century; Norway and Denmark

(60) Second Third of the 17th Century; Switzerland

(61) Mid-17th Century; France

(62) Last Third of the 17th Century; France

(63)   17th Century; Strasbourg

(64)   Late 17th and Early 18th Centuries

(65)   17th and 18th Centuries; Russia

(66)   17th and Early 18th Centuries; Turks

(67)   Egyptians, Moors, Turks

(68)   First Third of the 18th Century

(69)   First Third of the 18th Century; Military Costume

(70)   Second Half of the 18th Century

(71)   Last Third of the 18th Century

(72)   First Half of the 18th Century; German and Austrian Armies

(73)   Second Half of the 18th Century; German and Austrian Armies

(74)   1770–1790; German Middle Class

(75)   Late 18th Century; Germany

(76)   Late 18th Century; Germany

(77)   Early 18th Century; Switzerland (Canton of Zurich)

(78)   Late 18th Century; Switzerland

(79)   Late 18th Century; Switzerland

(80)   Late 18th Century; Switzerland

(81)   Late 18th Century; France Just Before the Revolution

(82)   Late 18th Century; French Republic

(83)   Late 18th Century; French Republic

(84)   Late 18th Century; Nun's Garb

(85)   Early 19th Century; Empire Style, Germany and France

(86)   Early 19th Century; Empire Style

(87)   Early 19th Century; Restoration

(88)   First Half of the 19th Century; Germany

(89)   Early 19th Century; Bavarian Army

(90)   Late 19th Century; Monastic Orders

(91)   Late 19th Century; Italian Folk Dress

(92)   Late 19th Century; Spanish Folk Dress

(93)   Late 19th Century; Dutch Folk Dress

(94)   Late 19th Century; Dutch Folk Dress

(95)   Late 19th Century; French Folk Dress (Brittany)

(96)   Late 19th Century; Alsatian Folk Dress

(97)   Late 19th Century; Swiss Folk Dress

(98)   Late 19th Century; North German Folk Dress

(99)   Late 19th Century; German Folk Dress (Former Grand-Duchy of Baden)

(100)   Late 19th Century; German Folk Dress (Baden)

(101)   Late 19th Century; German Folk Dress (Baden)

(102)   Late 19th Century; German Folk Dress (Former Kingdom of Bavaria)

(103)   Late 19th Century; German Folk Dress (Bavaria)

(104)   Late 19th Century; Tyrolean Folk Dress

(105)   Late 19th Century; Tyrolean Folk Dress

(106)   Late 19th Century; Tyrolean Folk Dress

(107)   Late 19th Century; Dalmatian Folk Dress

(108)   Late 19th Century; Folk Dress in European Turkey (Now Parts of Albania, Yugoslavia, Bulgaria and Greece)

(109)   Late 19th Century; Russian Folk Dress

(110)   Late 19th Century; Near East

(111)   Late 19th Century; Egypt

(112)   Late 19th Century; Caucasus

(113)   Late 19th Century; Central Asia

(114)   Late 19th Century; Afghanistan

(115)   Late 19th Century; Tibet and Kashmir

(116)   Late 19th Century; India and Malaysia

(117)   Late 19th Century (1880); Ceylon

(118)   Late 19th Century; Ceylon, Java, Siam

(119)   Late 19th Century (1886); Siam and Burma

(120)   Late 19th Century; Burma and Indo-China

(121)   Late 19th Century; East Indies

(122)   Late 19th Century (1880); Chinese in Malaysia

(123)   Late 19th Century; Japan

(124)   Late 19th Century; Asiatic Russia

(125)   Late 19th Century; Asia

PLATE 1
ANCIENT NEAR EAST

Mede nobility

Assyrian king

Assyrian high priest

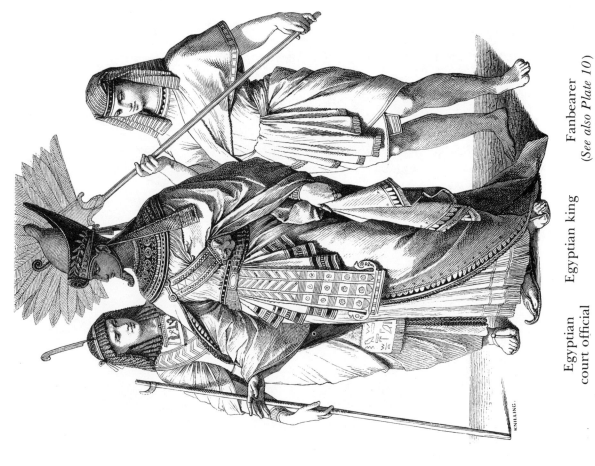

Egyptian
court official   Egyptian king   Fanbearer
                                       (See also Plate 10)

Egyptian queen with two noblewomen

PLATE 2
ANCIENT NEAR EAST

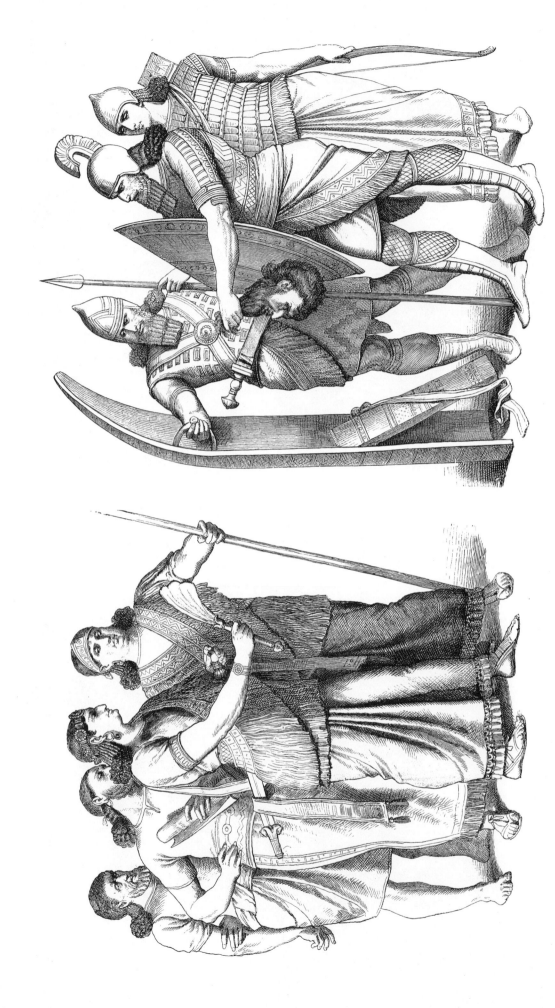

Archer

Soldier with small shield

Assyrian soldier with
standing shield

Assyrian noblemen

Commoner   Assyrian court official

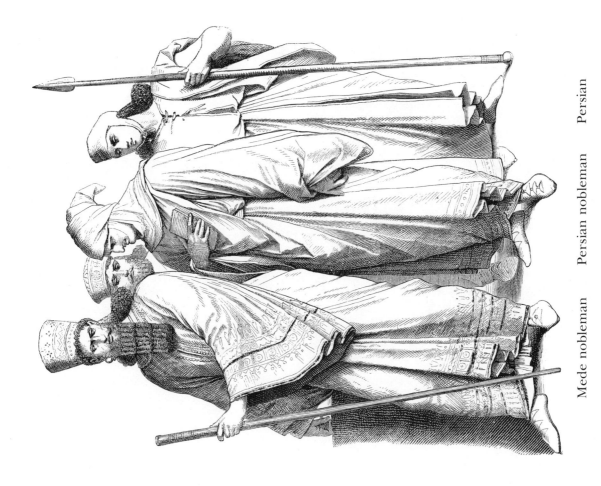

Mede nobleman   Persian nobleman   Persian

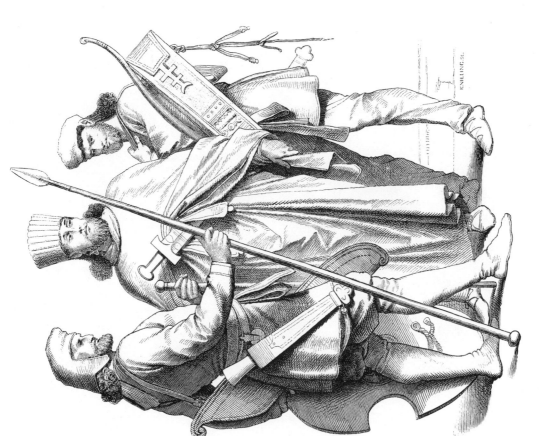

Persian nobleman with two Persian soldiers

PLATE 3
ANCIENT GREECE

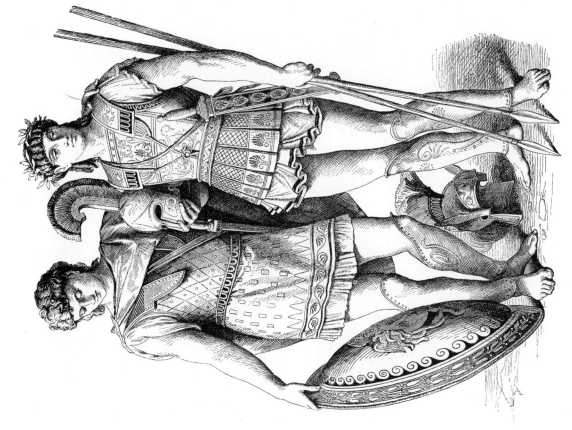

Captains

Priestess   Noblewomen

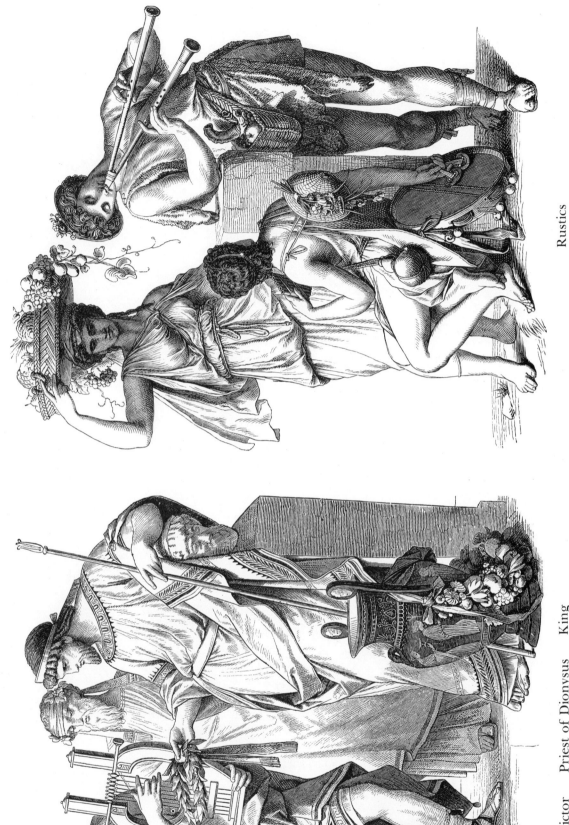

Olympic victor   Priest of Dionysus   King

Rustics

PLATE 4
ANCIENT ROME

Germanic standard-bearer   Roman general   Soldiers

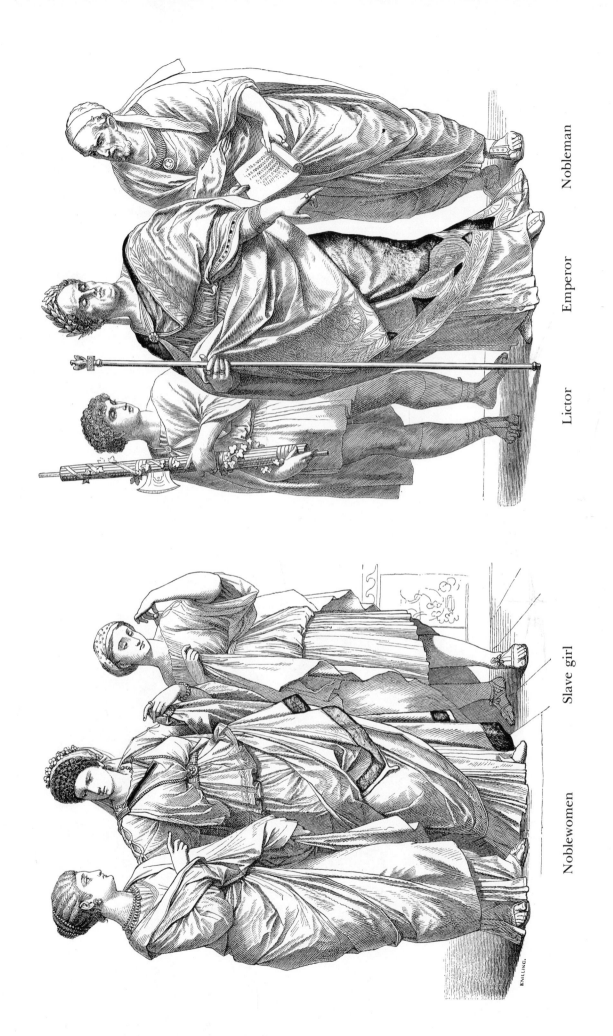

Nobleman

Emperor

Lictor

Noblewomen

Slave girl

KNILING.

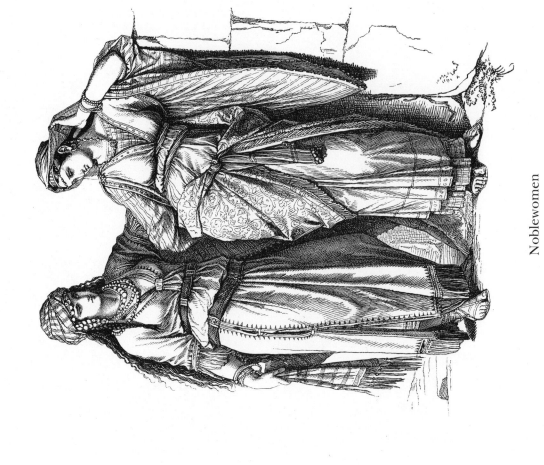

Noblewomen

PLATE 5
ANCIENT JUDAEA

Jewish noblemen

Levites

High priest

King

Soldiers

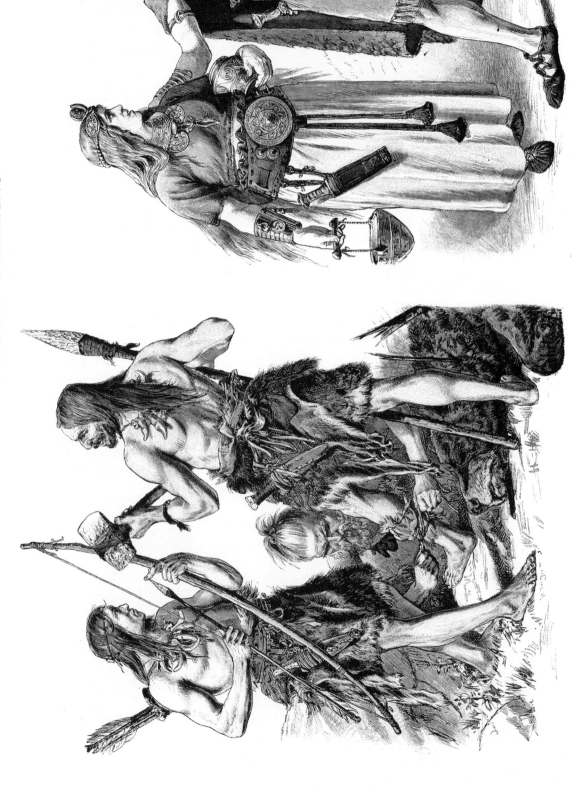

PLATE 6

ANCIENT GERMANS

In the Bronze Age

In the Stone Age

3rd to 4th centuries A.D.

At the beginning of the Christian Era

PLATE 7
4TH TO 6TH CENTURIES

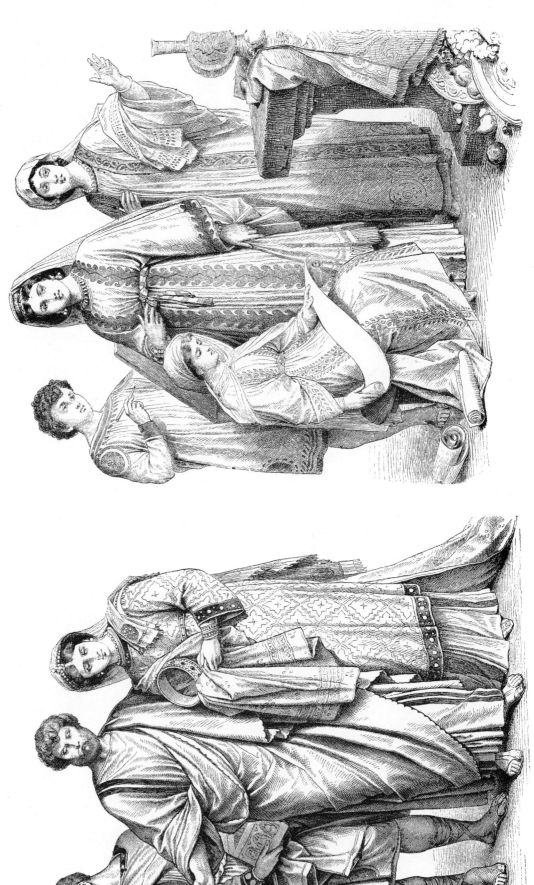

Christians

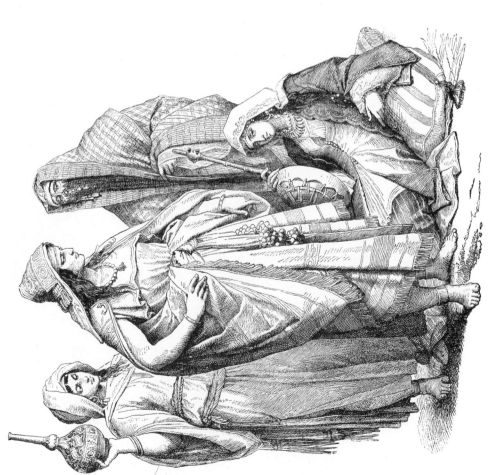

Arabs

PLATE 8

BYZANTINE EMPIRE

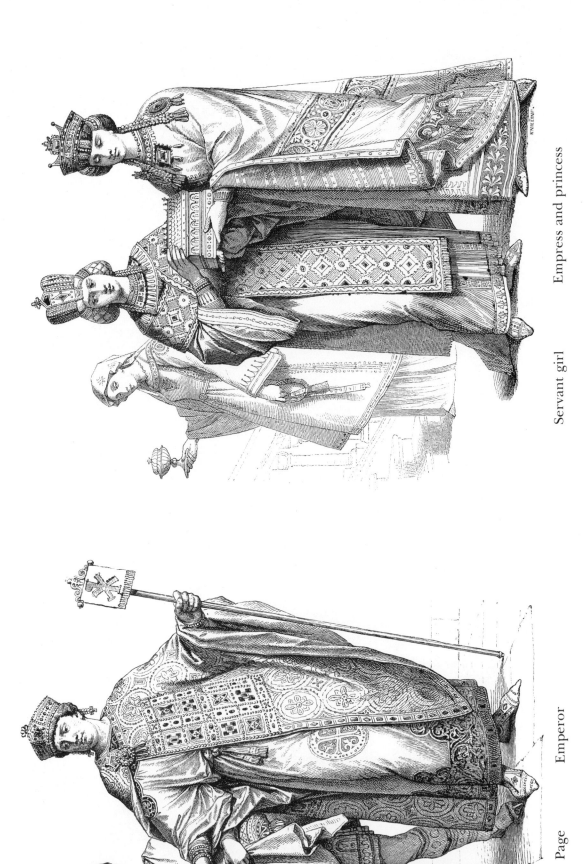

Servant girl   Empress and princess

Page   Emperor

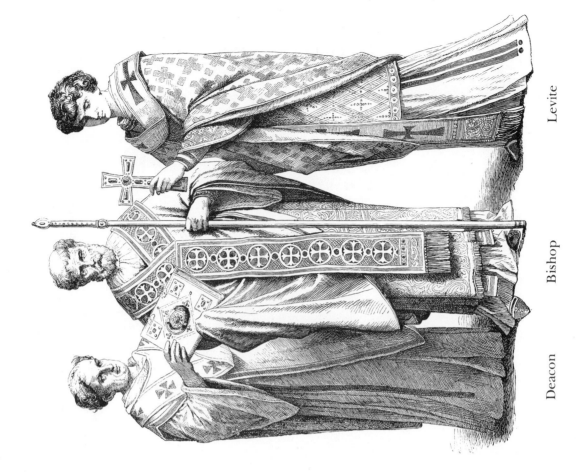

Levite

Bishop

Deacon

Soldier and chancellor

PLATE 9

6TH CENTURY; BYZANTINE EMPIRE

Early 6th century

Emperor Justinian (482–565)   Empress Theodora (d. 548)

Retinue of Empress Theodora, 547 A.D.

PLATE 10

5TH TO 10TH CENTURIES
(AND ANCIENT EGYPT)

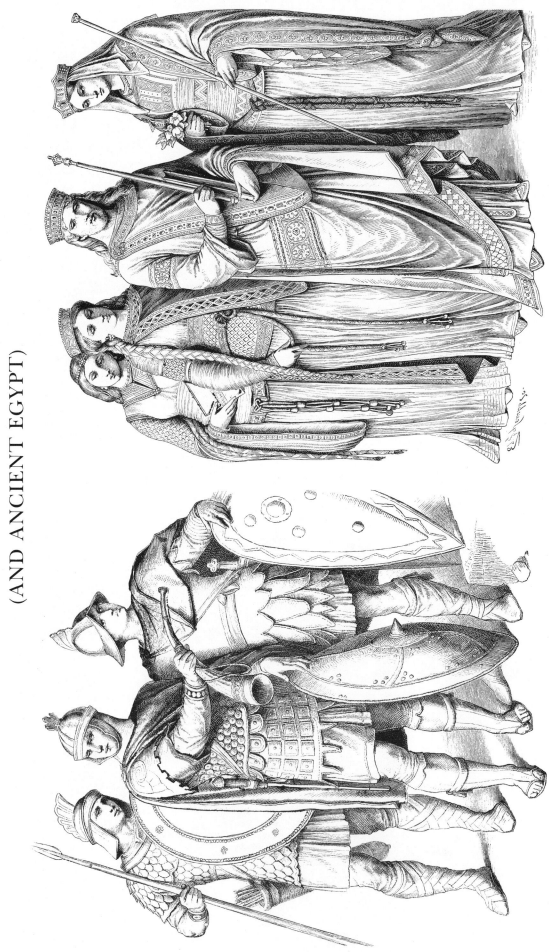

Charlemagne

Frankish ladies

Soldiers of the Eastern Roman Empire

Charioteer

Egyptian king
in battle garb

Egyptian soldiers

Frankish court dress

PLATE 11
700–800; CAROLINGIANS

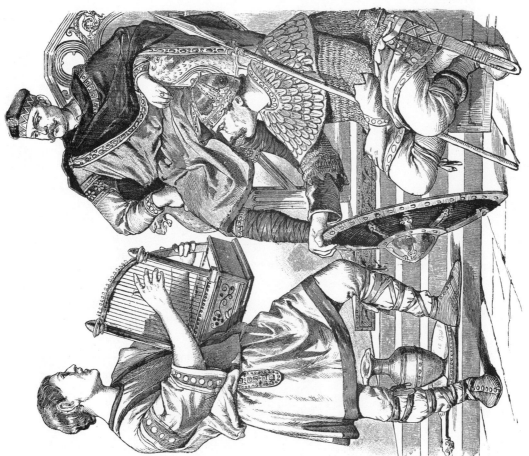

PLATE 12
10TH CENTURY

Frankish noblewomen

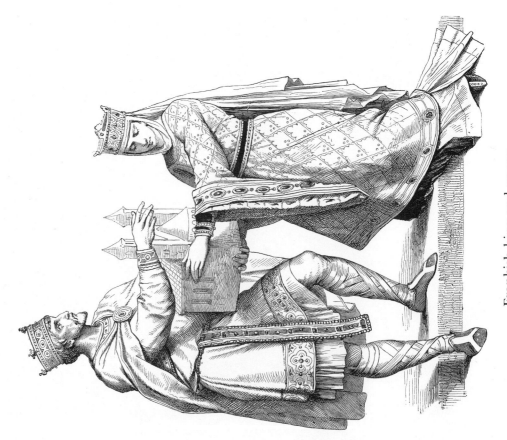

Frankish king and queen

Frankish bishop · Emperor Henry II

King Charles the Bald

PLATE 13
11TH CENTURY

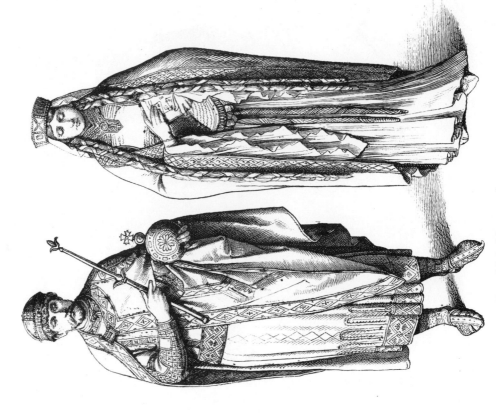

Frankish king and queen

Monk   Occidental bishop   Priest

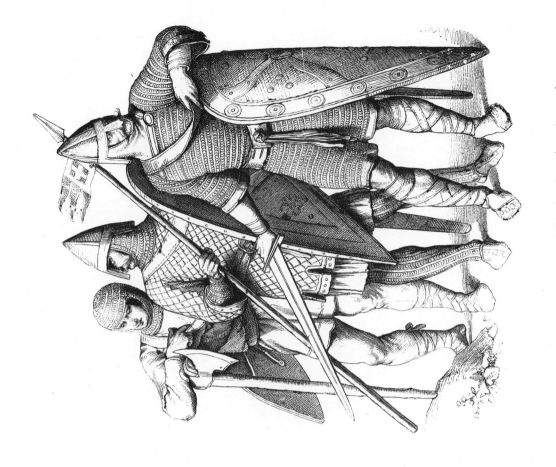

Knights and common soldier in the First Crusade

Norman ladies

Norman noblewoman

PLATE 14

12TH CENTURY

German noblewomen   German middle-class woman

Servant   Pope of Rome   King

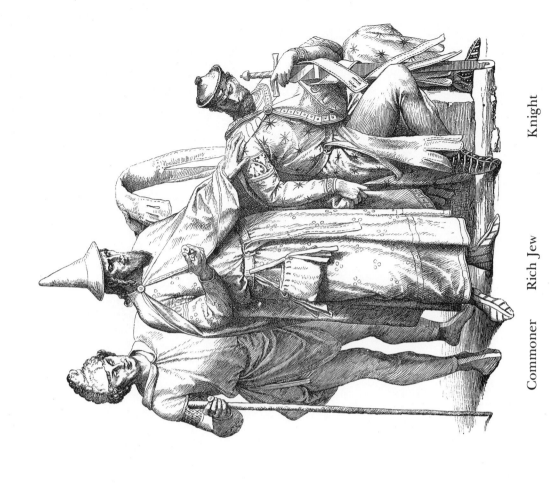

Commoner   Rich Jew   Knight

Squire and knight in the First Crusade

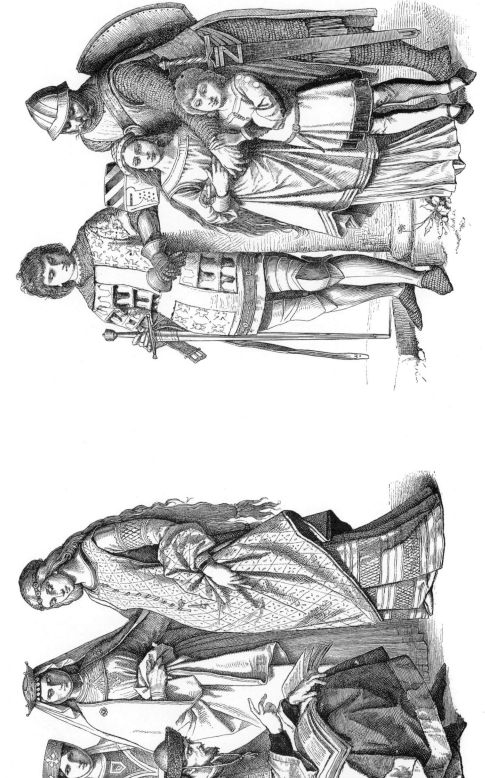

PLATE 15

13TH CENTURY

Family of a German knight

German prince   German ladies

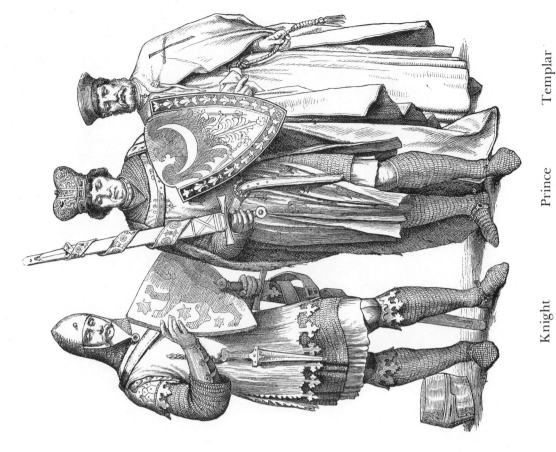

Templar

Prince

Knight

Italian scholars

German middle-class
woman

PLATE 16

12TH & 13TH CENTURIES;
MILITARY-RELIGIOUS ORDERS

Female and male members of the Order of St. John of Jerusalem (Hospitallers)

Templars

Master and Knight of the Teutonic Order

PLATE 17
14TH CENTURY

Townsman

Nobleman

Knight in hunting garb

German chatelaine

Nobleman

Page

Prince

English princess

Ladies-in-waiting

PLATE 18

14TH CENTURY

Princess and lady-in-waiting

Prince and knight

German patricians

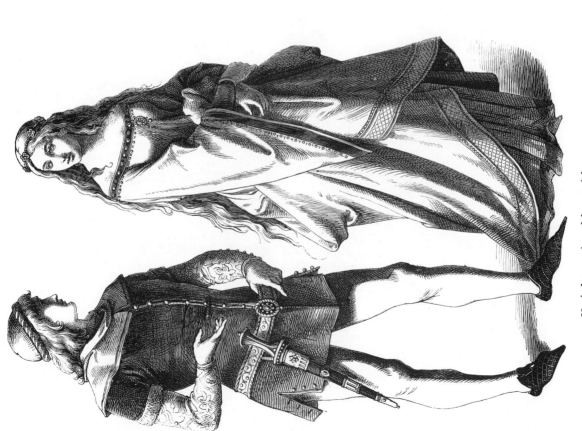

Knight and noble maiden

PLATE 19
14TH CENTURY; ENGLAND

1376 (middle-class garb)

1365

1390

1350

1330

1365

1330–1370

1350 (merchants)   1350–1360 (nobleman)

PLATE 20
14TH CENTURY; GERMANY

Heinrich of
Seinsheim, 1360

Count of
Katzenellenbogen,
1315

Count of Orlamünde
(mid-century)

Günther von Schwarzburg,
King of Germany, 1349

Knightly dress
(2nd half of century)

Konrad of Bikenbach, 1393   Weikhard Frosch, 1378
Gudela of Holzhausen, 1371

Rudolph of Sachsenhausen, 1370   Battle garb (2nd half of century)

PLATE 21

SECOND HALF OF THE 14TH
CENTURY; ITALY

Soldiers

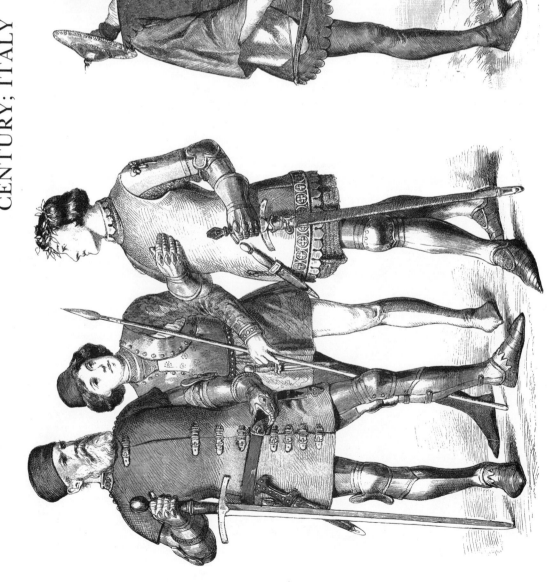

Vittore Pisani,
Venetian admiral
(d. 1380)

Squire

Neapolitan knight

Young man   Roman senator   Venetian nobleman

Girl   Noblewoman   Lady of Siena

PLATE 22

FIRST HALF OF THE
15TH CENTURY

German court dress

Burgundian court dress

Peasant   Townsman   Judge

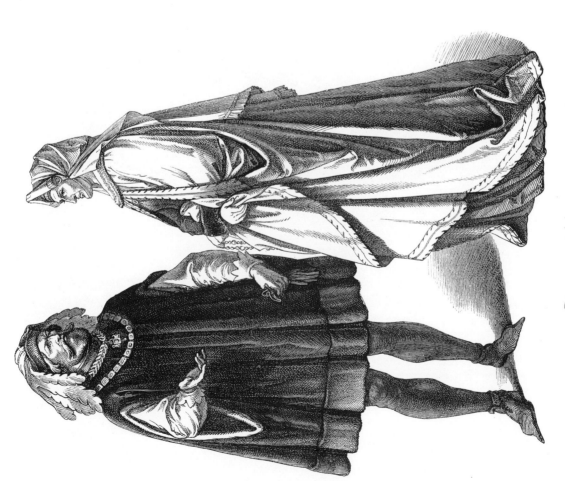

German patricians

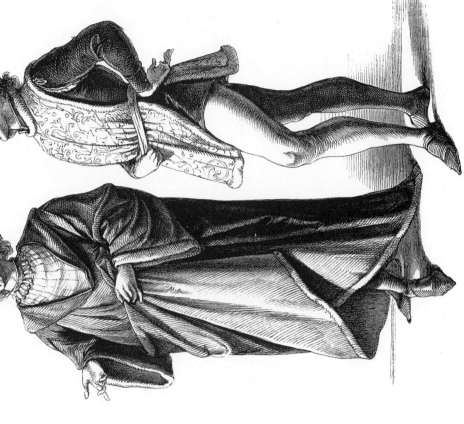

PLATE 23

FIRST HALF OF THE
15TH CENTURY

Florentine nobility

French noblemen

German noblewomen

PLATE 24

SECOND HALF OF THE
15TH CENTURY

French costumes

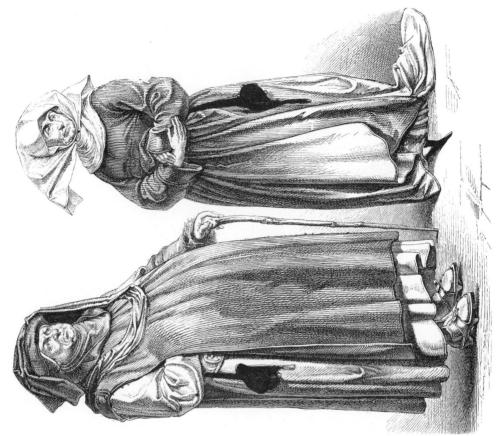

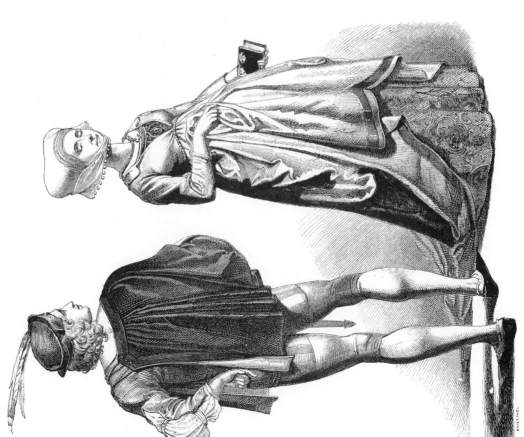

German patricians

PLATE 25

15TH CENTURY; ITALY

Podesta   Sexton   Soldier

Mid-century   Apothecary
(1st half of century)

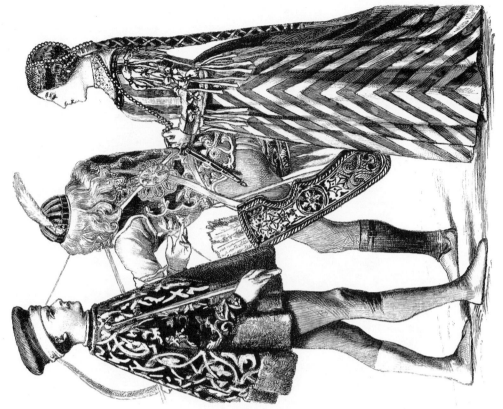

Lord of Rimini   1488   Beatrice d'Este, 1490

Mid-century   End of century

PLATE 26

15TH CENTURY; FRANCE

1460–1480

Charles the Bold, 1477

Women's dress, 1480

1460–1480

PLATE 27

15TH CENTURY; FRANCE
AND ENGLAND

France, 1470

England, 1400

Henry VII
of England
(1456–1509)

Duke of
Suffolk, 1470

Henry VI,
1471

Duchess of
Suffolk, 1470

England (1st third of century)

PLATE 28

MID-15TH CENTURY; BURGUNDY

Charles the Bold

PLATE 29

SECOND HALF OF THE 15TH CENTURY;
BURGUNDY AND HOLLAND

Burgundy, 1470

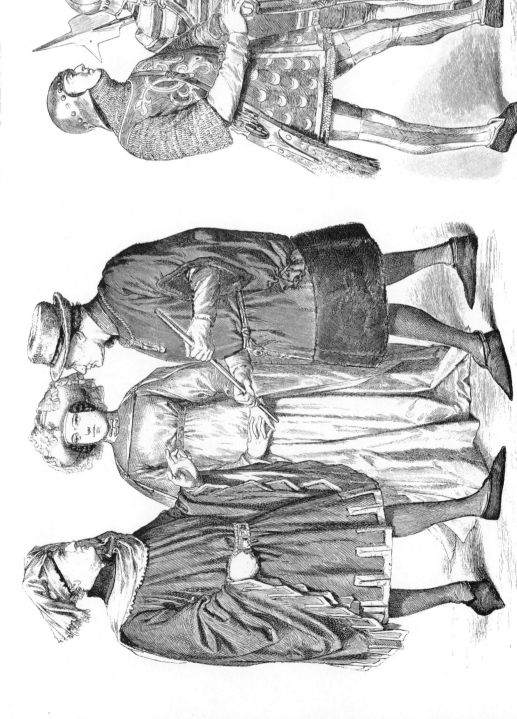

Holland, 1470–1485

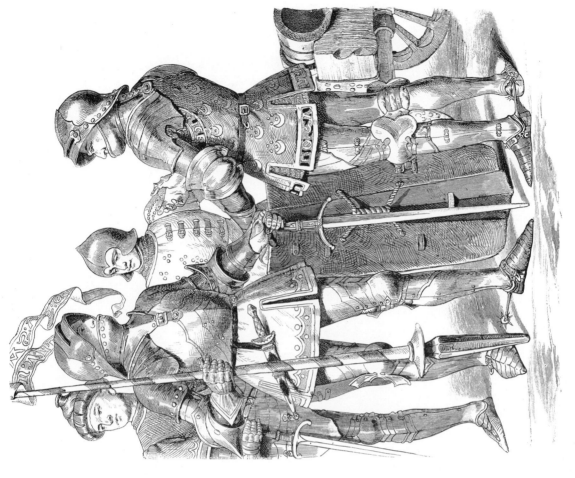

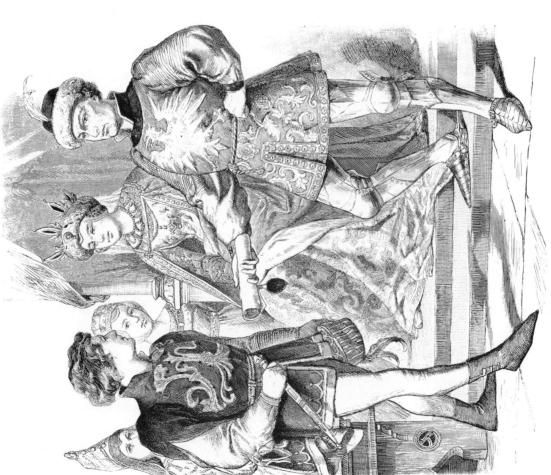

Burgundy, 1470

PLATE 30

15TH CENTURY; GERMANY

Philipp of Ingelheim,
1431

Martin of
Seinsheim, 1434

About 1410

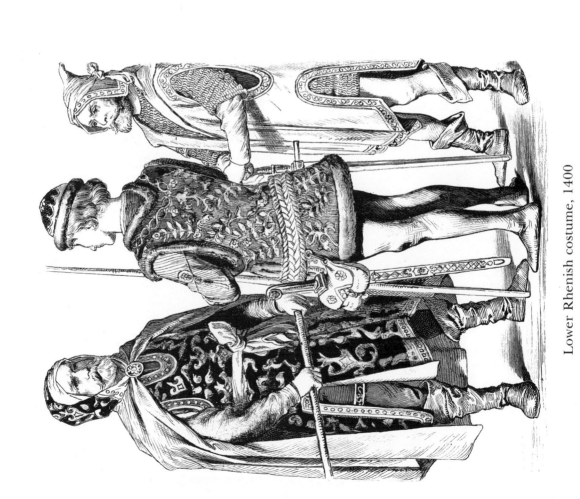

Lower Rhenish costume, 1400

Mid-century

Lady's costume
(mid-century)

Townsman of
Ravensburg, 1429

Knight of
Stettenberg, 1428

PLATE 31

15TH CENTURY; SWISS
MILITARY COSTUME

Boy   Captain   Executioner

Standard-bearer   Piper   Drummer

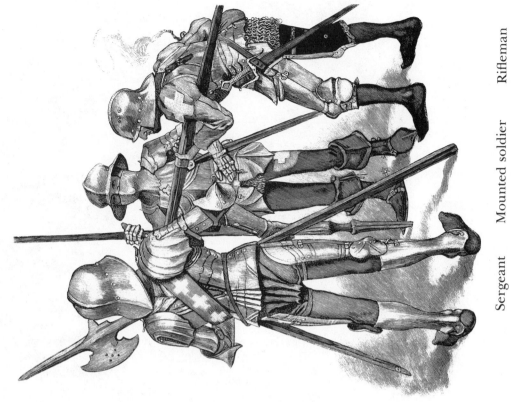

Sergeant   Mounted soldier   Rifleman

Infantrymen

PLATE 32
15TH AND 16TH CENTURIES

Prince and princess (1st third of 16th century)

German knight and noblewoman (mid-15th century)

Knight and noblewoman (1st third of 16th century)

German townswoman and armed townsman (1st third of 16th century)

PLATE 33

FIRST THIRD OF THE
16TH CENTURY

German magistrate and knight

French noblewoman and page

German patrician women

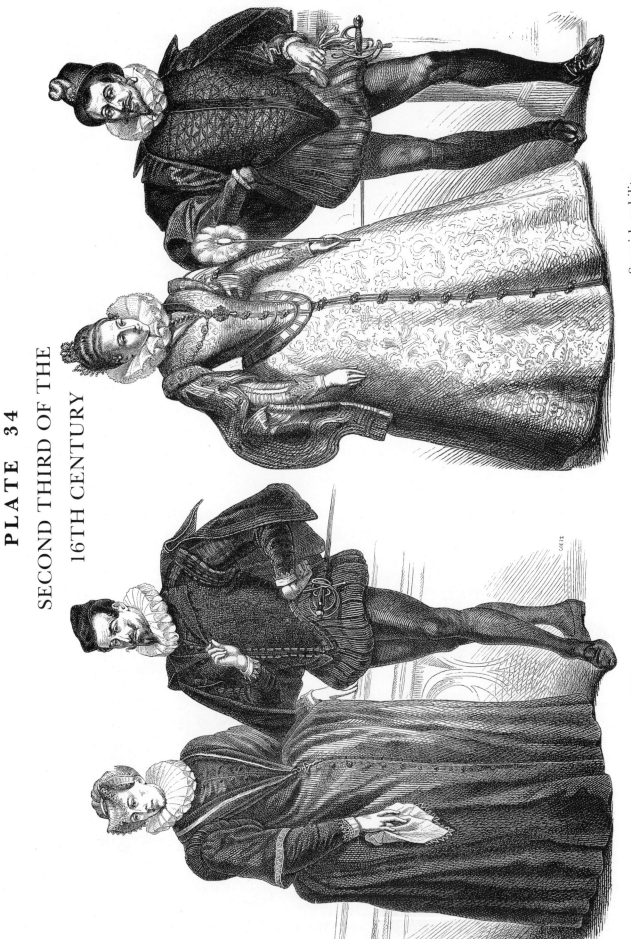

PLATE 34

SECOND THIRD OF THE
16TH CENTURY

Spanish nobility

German nobility

French court dress

PLATE 35

LAST THIRD OF THE 16TH CENTURY

French nobility

German nobility (Palatinate)

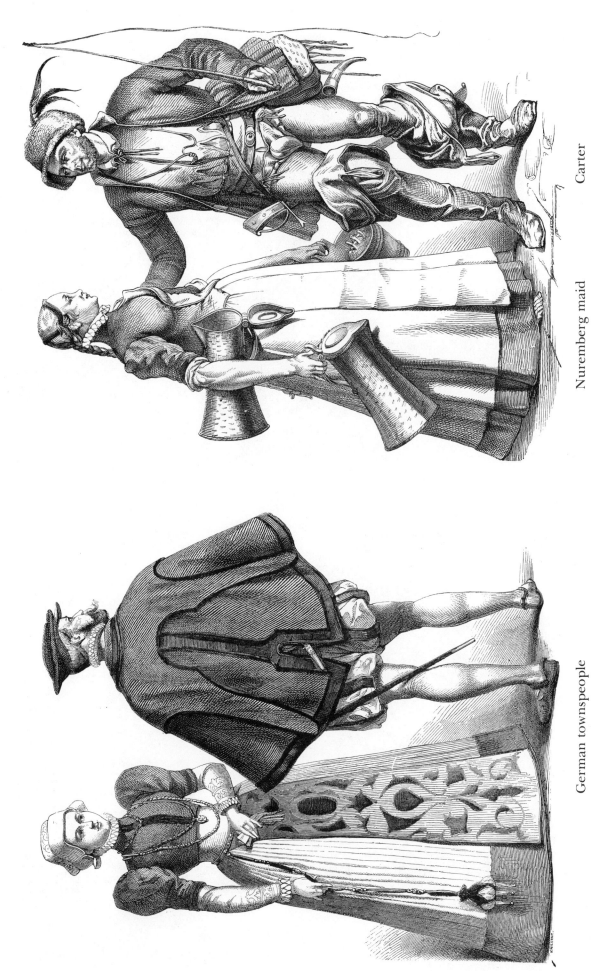

Carter

Nuremberg maid

German townspeople

PLATE 36

FIRST THIRD OF THE
16TH CENTURY; GERMANY

Patricians

Nobility

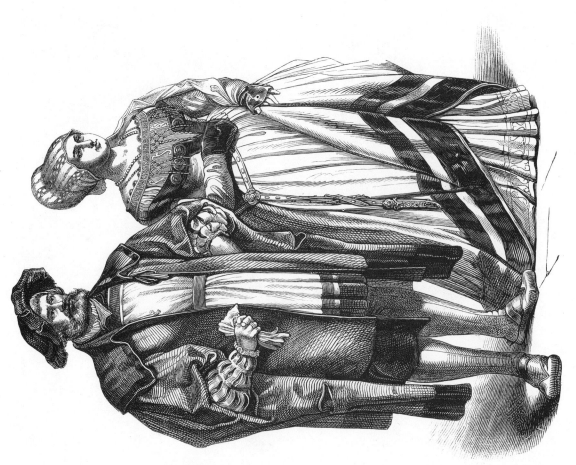

Patricians

PLATE 37

FIRST THIRD OF THE
16TH CENTURY; GERMANY

Soldiers

Townspeople

Townspeople

Soldiers

PLATE 38

FIRST THIRD OF THE
16TH CENTURY; GERMANY

Mountain huntsmen with snowshoes

Scholar and townswoman

Peasants

Soldiers

PLATE 39

FIRST THIRD OF THE 16TH CENTURY;

GERMAN MILITARY COSTUME

Standard-bearer

Drummer

Soldiers

Lieutenant

Captain

Sergeant

Piper

PLATE 40

MID-16TH CENTURY; GERMANY

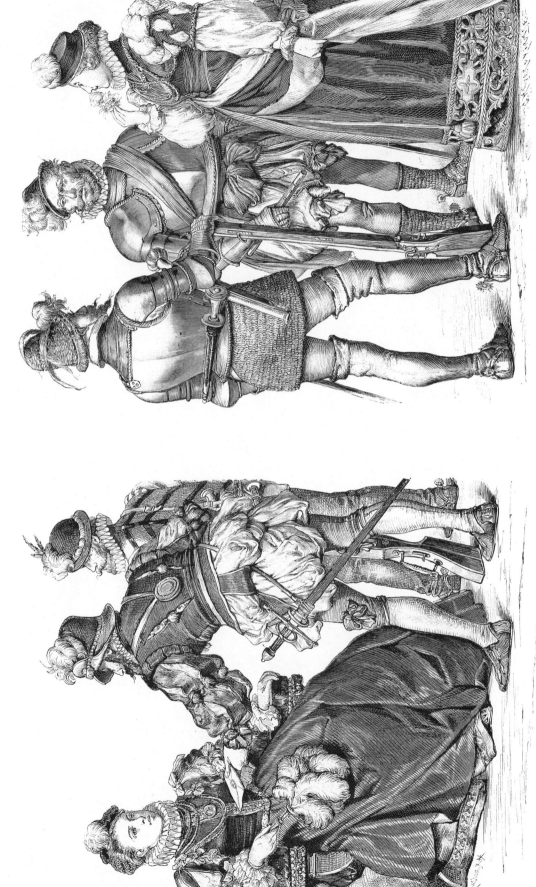

Lady, 1560

Cavalry general
under Charles V

Cavalryman

1565–1570

Noblewoman

Standard-bearer

About 1570

Itinerant musician

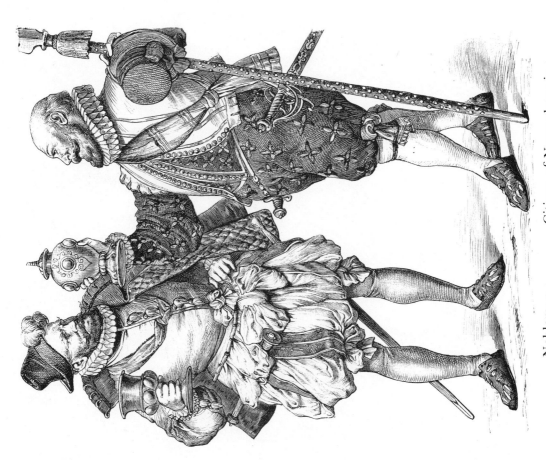

Nobleman,
about 1570

Citizen of Nuremberg in
festive attire, 1588

PLATE 41

LATE 16TH CENTURY; GERMANY

Pomerania, 1590

Woman from
Rostock

Councilman and lady
from Wismar, 1590

Man from
Dithmarschen

Girl from Ockholm   Man and woman
from Pomerania, 1590

Merchant and peasants from Rostock, 1590

PLATE 42

LATE 16TH CENTURY; FRISIA

Woman from Stapelholm on the Eider

Man from the North Sea coast, 1590

Man from Stapelholm

Man from the North Sea coast

Dithmarschen, 1590

Man from Eiderstadt

Man and woman
from the island of Föhr, 1590

Man from Ockholm

Man and woman from
the island of Sylt, 1590

Man from
Haderstedt

PLATE 43

16TH CENTURY; FRANCE

Antoine Bourbon,
King of Navarre,
father of Henry IV
(1518–1562)

Charles IX in
full regalia

Francis II

Francis II
(1543–1560)

Elizabeth, daughter
of Henry II,
as a bride
(1545–1568)

Francis II
as Dauphin

Claude de Lorraine,
Duke of Aumale, 1515–1550

Henri d'Albret, King of
Navarre (1505–1555)

Charles IX (1550–1574)

PLATE 44

16TH CENTURY; POLAND AND RUSSIA

Armored cavalryman

Lancer

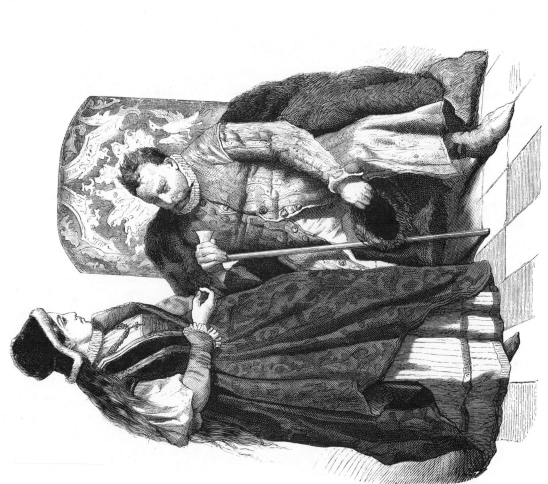

Polish lady and nobleman in national dress

Polish nobility in court dress

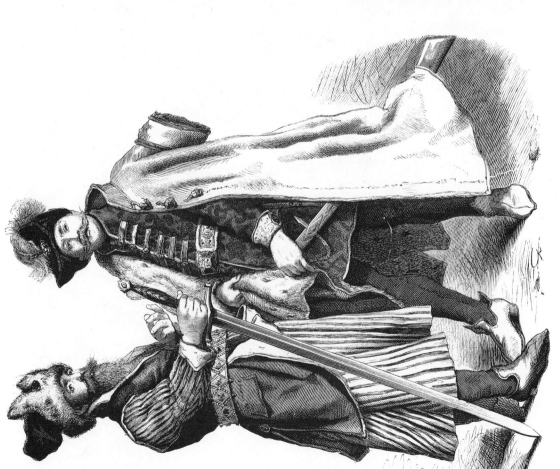

Russian aristocrat   Polish nobleman

PLATE 45
16TH CENTURY; ITALY

Florence and Padua

Rome and Siena

Venetian doge and dogaressa

Venetian senator and noblewoman

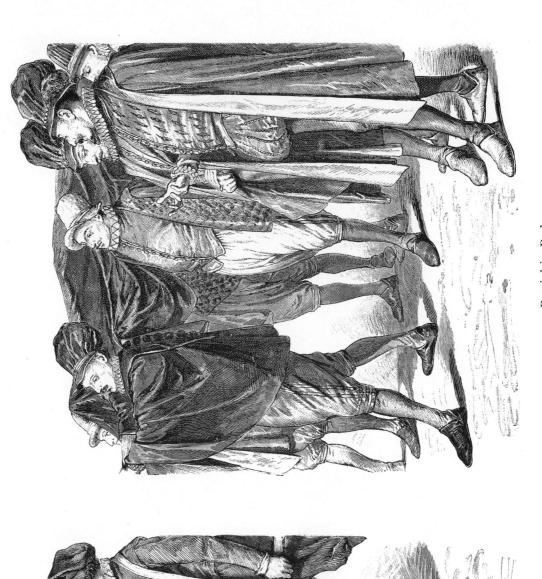

Burial in Padua

PLATE 46
LATE 16TH CENTURY
(1583); ITALY

Neapolitans

Venice   Milan   Florence

Students in Padua   Peasant woman

PLATE 47
16TH CENTURY; ENGLAND

London merchant   Cavalier,   Lady of
1550–1600   Queen Elizabeth's court

Henry VIII (1509–1546)   Anne of Cleves, 1525

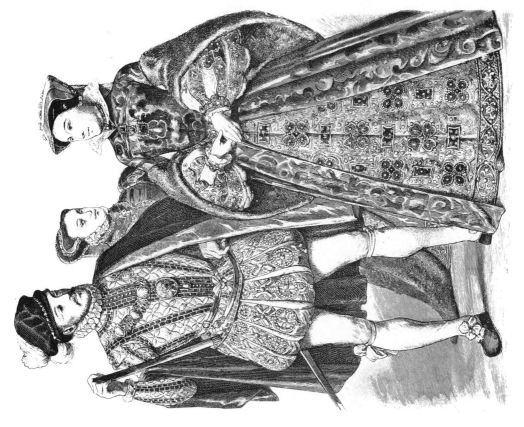

Lord Darnley, husband of Queen Mary of Scotland, 1566

Marchioness of Dorset

Queen Mary of Scotland, 1566

Mary of Scotland, late 16th century

Earl Douglas of Angus, 1570

Edward VI, 1550

PLATE 48

16TH AND 17TH
CENTURIES; ENGLAND

Officer

London, 1590: Merchant and wife

Noblewomen, London, 1590

1640:
Townswoman   Lady in   Lord Mayor's   Matron
              street dress wife

London, 1590:   Servant woman   Townswoman
Merchant's wife

PLATE 49

16TH AND 17TH CENTURIES

1640: Bohemian woman   Girl from Prague   Woman from Spain

1640: Dutch skipper's wife   Woman from Amsterdam   Dutch woman at home   Woman from Antwerp

Poland, 1590–1660

1640: English   Woman   Woman   Woman
noblewoman   from Paris   from Rouen   from Dieppe

PLATE 50

16TH AND 17TH CENTURIES;
ECCLESIASTICAL VESTMENTS

Subdeacon in alb
and colored stole

Acolyte in
surplice

Deacon with dalmatic
and alb

Prelate

Cardinal

Chamberlain

Bishop in chasuble

Bishop in pluvial

Swiss guard

Pope in
ceremonial dress

Pope in
domestic dress

PLATE 51

FIRST HALF OF THE
17TH CENTURY

Soldiers, 1630–1650

Princely dress, 1625–1640

Noblemen, 1625–1640

Englishman, 1638–1640   Fleming, 1640–1650

PLATE 52

SECOND THIRD OF THE

17TH CENTURY

German nobility

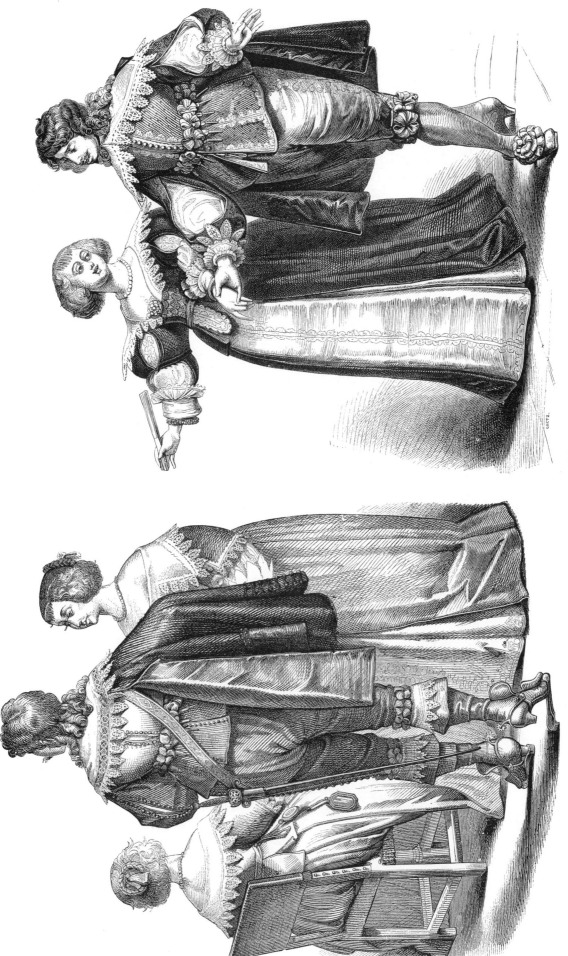

French nobility

PLATE 53

SECOND THIRD OF THE 17TH CENTURY

Nobility

Musketeer and pikeman in the Thirty Years' War

Dutch nobility

French cavalrymen

PLATE 54

LAST THIRD OF THE
17TH CENTURY

French nobility in court dress

French cavaliers

Dutch middle-class dress

PLATE 55

17TH CENTURY; ENGLAND

William Villiers,   Royalist soldier,   Nobleman,
Viscount of   1649   1649
Grandison, 1640

Anne, Countess of   Courtier of   Duke of
Chesterfield,   Charles II,   Newcastle,
1640   1665   1646

James,
Marquess of
Hamilton, 1620

Townsman

Frances,
Duchess of
Richmond, 1620

1625

Slingsby Bethel,
Sheriff of London,
1680

Cavalier of
Charles II,
1680

Duchess of
Cleveland, 1675

PLATE 56

FIRST THIRD OF THE 17TH CENTURY; NETHERLANDS

Middle-class dress in the Netherlands

Spanish court dress in the Netherlands

Dutch aristocrats

Dutch artist and page

PLATE 57

FIRST THIRD OF THE 17TH
CENTURY; GERMANY

Soldiers

Middle-class dress

Soldiers

PLATE 58

MID-17TH CENTURY; GERMAN LANDS

Strasbourg   Strasbourg   Basel

Munich   Nuremberg   Vienna

Servant girl   Townswoman   Matron
                from Cologne

Frankfurt am Main   Palatinate   Swabian woman

PLATE 59

FIRST THIRD OF THE 17TH CENTURY;
NORWAY AND DENMARK

Norway: Aristocrat and wife   Countrywoman

Denmark: Nobility

Denmark: Upford   Dithmarschen   Eiderstadt

Denmark: Townswoman   Merchant   Woman from Stappelhall

PLATE 60

SECOND THIRD OF THE 17TH
CENTURY; SWITZERLAND

Peasants

Young townsman   Bride   Young townswoman

Mourning   Chief bailiff   Village mayor

Churchgoing dress   Bailiff   Messenger

PLATE 61
MID-17TH CENTURY; FRANCE

Peasant   Townswoman   Merchant

Noblemen

Lady in mourning

Noblewomen

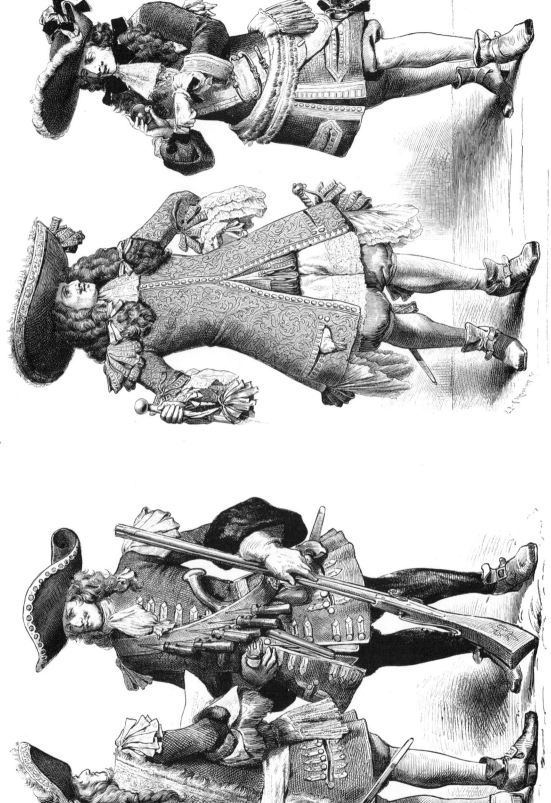

PLATE 62

LAST THIRD OF THE 17TH
CENTURY; FRANCE

Infantry officer

Officer of the palace guard

Officer and musketeer of the guard

Officer

Nobleman

Mounted gendarme

Peasants

PLATE 63

17TH CENTURY; STRASBOURG

1670: Consul

Councilman

1670: Woman
with broad cap

Woman in
winter dress

Woman in
mourning

1670–1690: Girls   Bride

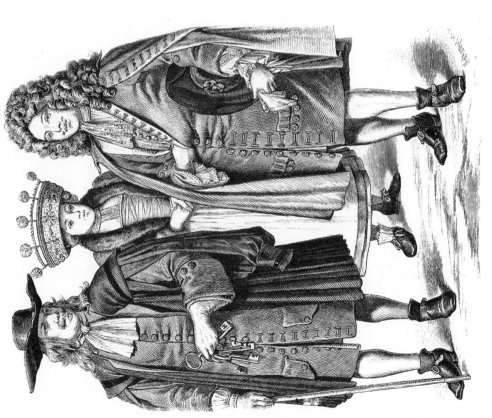

1670: Tower warden   Peasant bride   Bridegroom

PLATE 64

LATE 17TH AND EARLY
18TH CENTURIES

Young dandy, 1670

Maria Anna of Bavaria
as Crown Princess of
France, court dress,
1679

Palace guard
(la manche)
of Louis XV
of France, 1724

Françoise Marie
de Bourbon,
Duchess of Orleans,
1702

Duchess of Portsmouth
(Louise de Kéroualle),
1694

Maria Anna
of Bavaria,
1694

Palace guard
1670

Hedwig Sophie, Princess
of Sweden, Duchess of
Holstein, 1700

Elizabeth of Brunswick,
1707

PLATE 65

17TH AND 18TH
CENTURIES; RUSSIA

Boyars

Boyarina

Boyar

Tsar

Boyar

Woman from Ryazan

Women's winter dress in Torshko

Princely dress   Women's summer dress   Woman from
                  in Torshko   Belosersk

PLATE 66

17TH AND EARLY 18TH
CENTURIES; TURKS

Soldiers

Street dress   Sultana   Sultan   Dancer

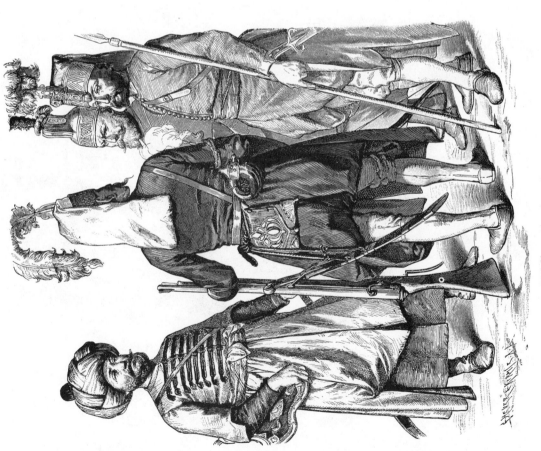

Soldiers

Soldiers (janissaries)

PLATE 67

EGYPTIANS, MOORS, TURKS

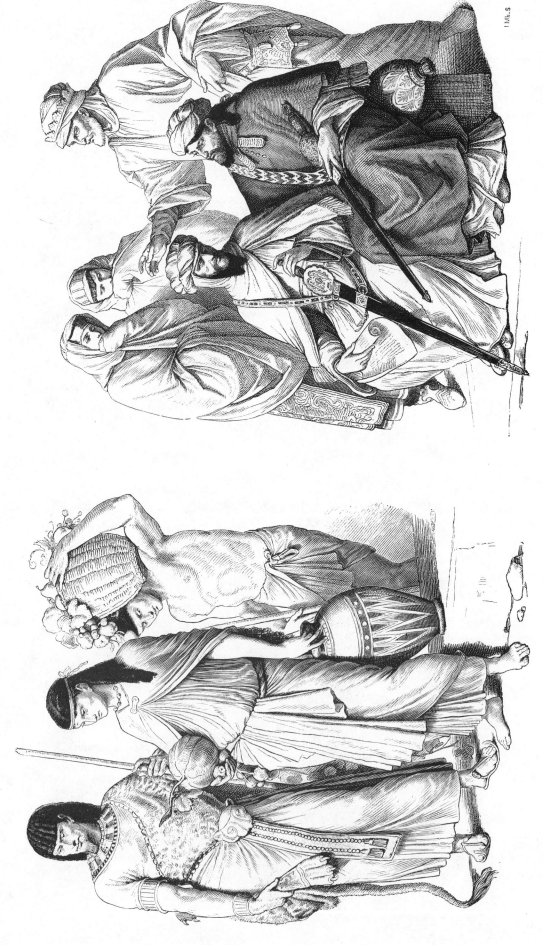

Moorish princes

Egyptian king (ancient)

Commoners

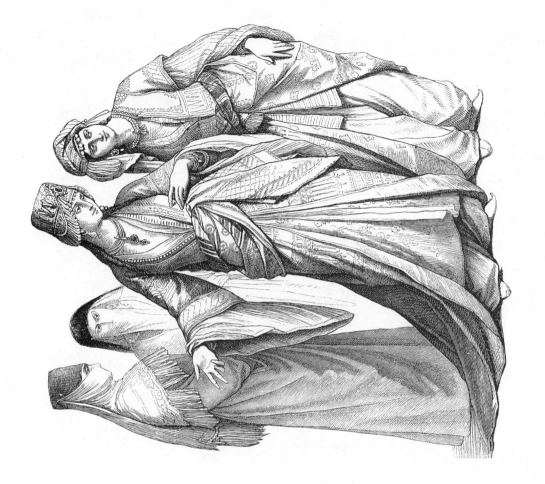

Turkish women

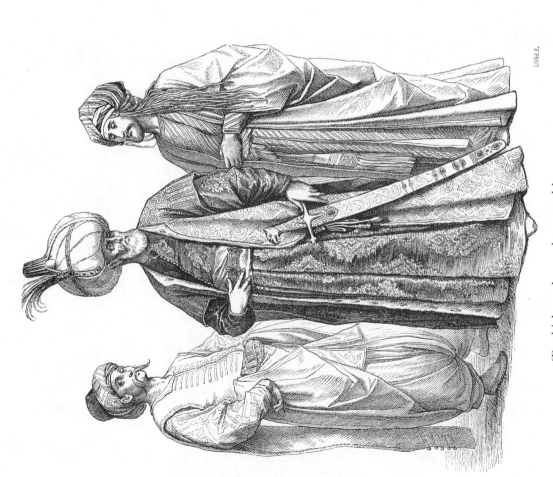

Turkish pasha and two noblemen

PLATE 68

FIRST THIRD OF THE
18TH CENTURY

Gentleman and lady of the court of Louis XIV

Noblewoman

French abbé

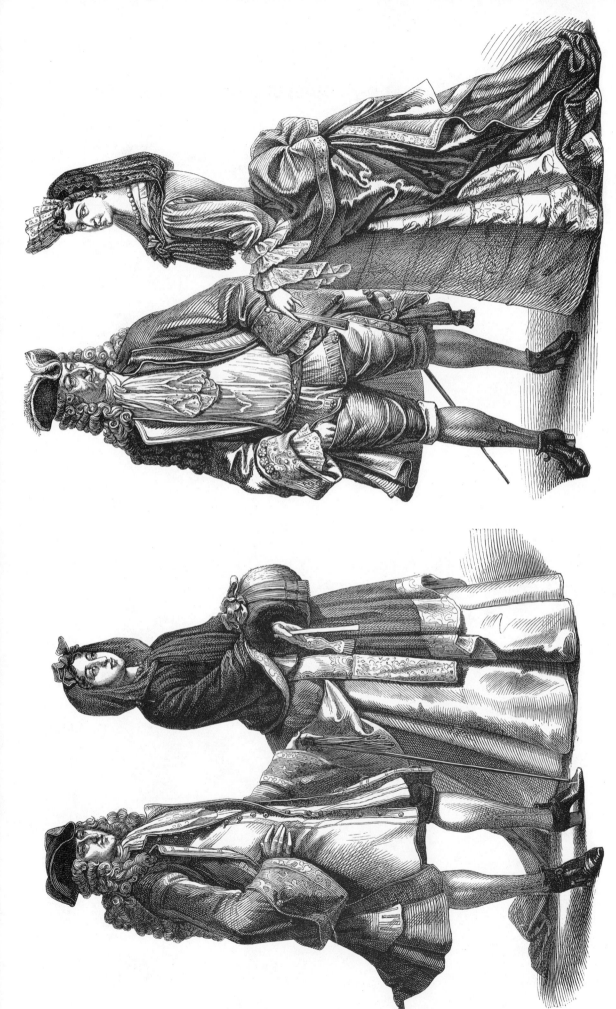

French gentleman and lady

German gentleman and lady

PLATE 69

FIRST THIRD OF THE 18TH CENTURY;
MILITARY COSTUME

Louis XV and French general, 1704–1730

French marshal and subaltern, 1704–1730

Austrian infantrymen, 1704–1710

Austrian cavalrymen, 1704–1710

PLATE 70

SECOND HALF OF THE 18TH CENTURY

Lady in hoopskirt

Dress before 1780

Dress of 1780

Servant girl in a contouche

Abbé

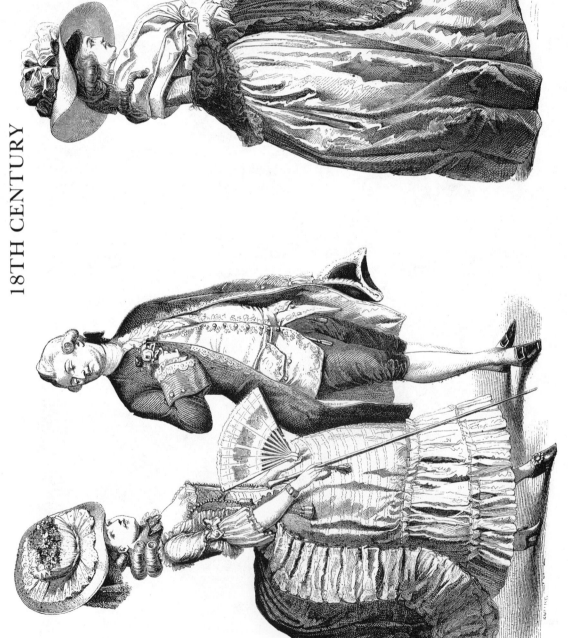

PLATE 71

LAST THIRD OF THE
18TH CENTURY

Germany at the time of *Werther* (ca. 1775)

France, 1780

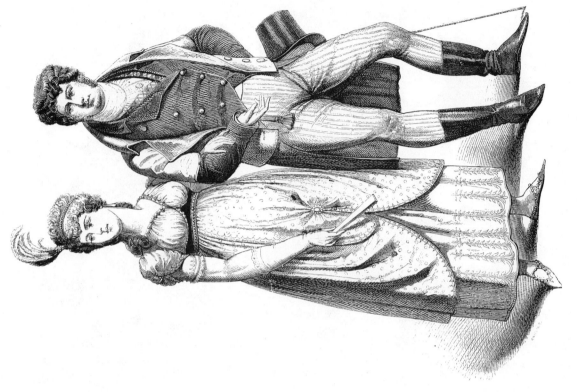

Germany, after 1800

French incroyables, 1794

PLATE 72

FIRST HALF OF THE 18TH CENTURY;
GERMAN AND AUSTRIAN ARMIES

Württemberg, Officer Drummer Sergeant
1724–1738:
Private

Württemberg, Cuirassier General
ca. 1730:
Grenadier

Austria, 1728

Army of the
Archbishop of
Konstanz,
1738: Officer
of grenadiers

Grenadier   Dragoon   Infantryman

PLATE 73

SECOND HALF OF THE 18TH CENTURY;

GERMAN AND
AUSTRIAN ARMIES

Austria, 1760–1775: Infantryman

Austria, 1760–1775: Hussar

Officer

Austria, 1760–1775: General

Prussia, 1760:   Cuirassier in   Mounted grenadier
Officer of hussars   Seydlitz' army   (private)

Prussia, 1760: Officer   Grenadier
of guard battalion

PLATE 74
1770–1790; GERMAN
MIDDLE CLASS

Frankfurt Vienna Karlsruhe

Mannheim German and French dress in Strasbourg

Ludwigsburg   Munich   Black Forest
peasant girl

Girl and woman from Augsburg

PLATE 75

LATE 18TH CENTURY;
GERMANY

1788

1793

Saxon army   Hessian
postmaster   postilion

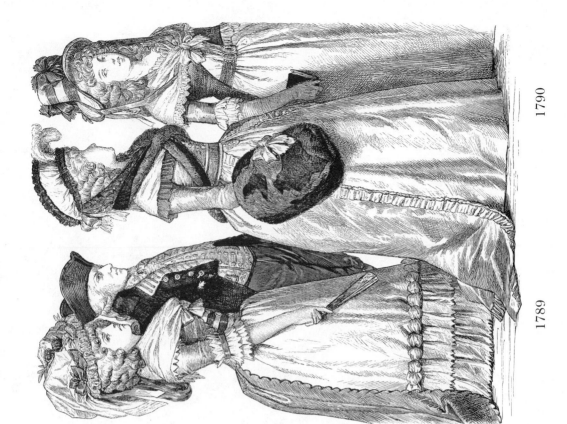

1790

1789

1792

1791

PLATE 76
LATE 18th CENTURY;
GERMANY

1799

1798

1787

Winter dress, 1795

Spring dress, 1794

1797

Woman from Berlin, 1796

PLATE 77

EARLY 18TH CENTURY; SWITZERLAND

(CANTON OF ZURICH)

Women's   Noblewoman   Girl's   Girl
ceremonial dress   in mourning   domestic attire   with "rose cap"

Student   Townsman   Councilman   Nobleman

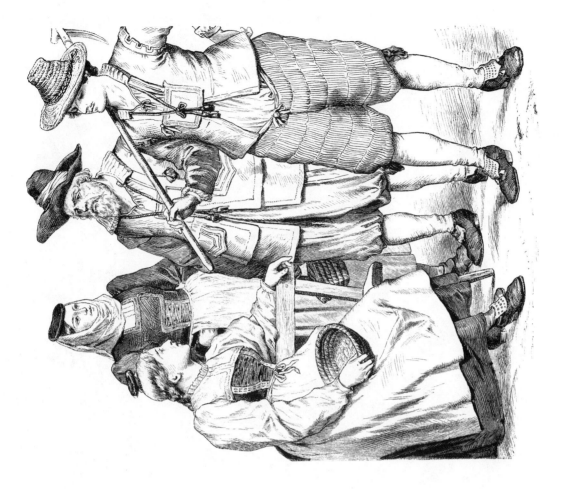

Peasants

Riding attire,
also worn at
weddings

Festive middle-
class women's
attire

Girls' and
women's
visiting dress

Churchgoing dress,
called *Hussegken*

PLATE 78
LATE 18TH CENTURY; SWITZERLAND

Zug   Schwyz

Solothurn   Lucerne

Wedding costume, Zurich

Valais

Solothurn

PLATE 79

LATE 18TH CENTURY;
SWITZERLAND

Unterwalden   Fribourg

District captain, Aargau   Aargau

Berne

Aargau   St. Gallen

PLATE 80
LATE 18TH CENTURY; SWITZERLAND

Best man and bride, Lucerne

St. Gallen   Zug   Zurich

Schaffhausen, festive dress
and winter dress

Ausser Rhoden,
Appenzell

Fribourg

PLATE 81

LATE 18TH CENTURY; FRANCE JUST
BEFORE THE REVOLUTION

1787   1792   1787

1778–1779   1774–1779   1778–1780

1784   1784   1781

1778–1780   1774–1779   1777–1780

PLATE 82

LATE 18TH CENTURY;
FRENCH REPUBLIC

Grenadier, 1795

Infantryman, 1799

Middle class, 1790–1792

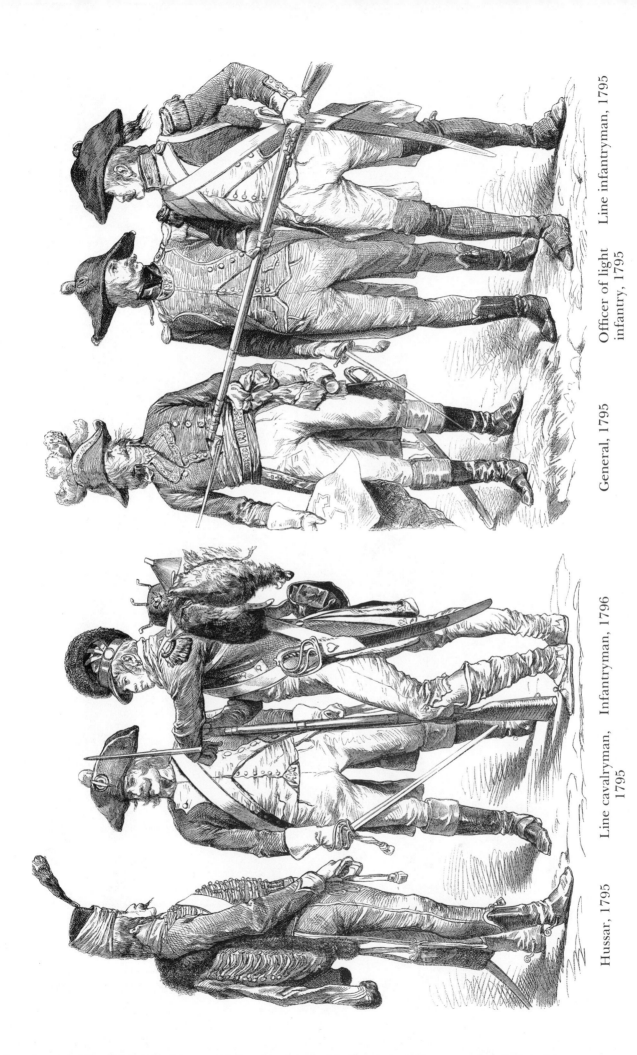

Line infantryman, 1795

Officer of light
infantry, 1795

General, 1795

Hussar, 1795

Line cavalryman,
1795

Infantryman, 1796

PLATE 83

LATE 18TH CENTURY; FRENCH REPUBLIC

Middle-class dress, 1796

1794–1799: Member of the   Gala dress of a member
Council of the Five Hundred   of the Directoire

Members of the Commune, 1793–1794

Generals, 1799–1800

PLATE 84

LATE 18TH CENTURY;
NUN'S GARB

Dominicans

Augustinians

Ursulines

Benedictines

PLATE 85

EARLY 19TH CENTURY;
EMPIRE STYLE, GERMANY AND FRANCE

1802   1803–1804

1809–1812

1808–1809

1802–1804

PLATE 86

EARLY 19th CENTURY; EMPIRE STYLE

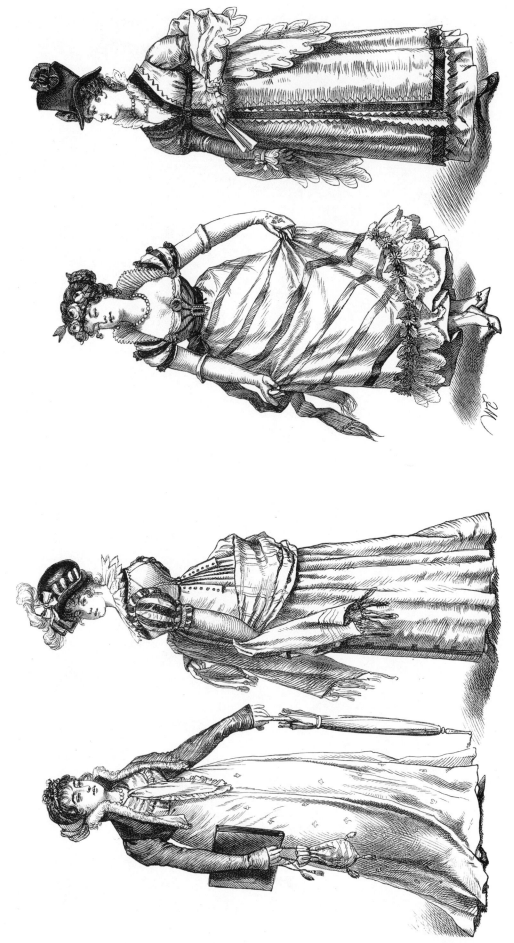

Lady with high hat

Lady in ball gown, 1805

Lady with a spencer

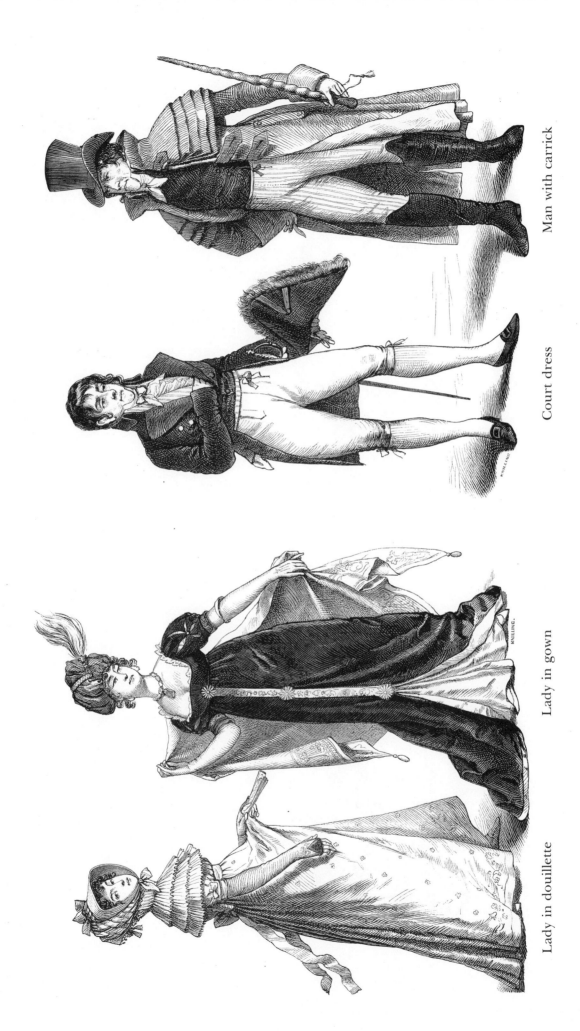

Man with carrick

Court dress

Lady in gown

Lady in douillette

PLATE 87

EARLY 19TH CENTURY;
RESTORATION

1818

1814

1819

1819

1818

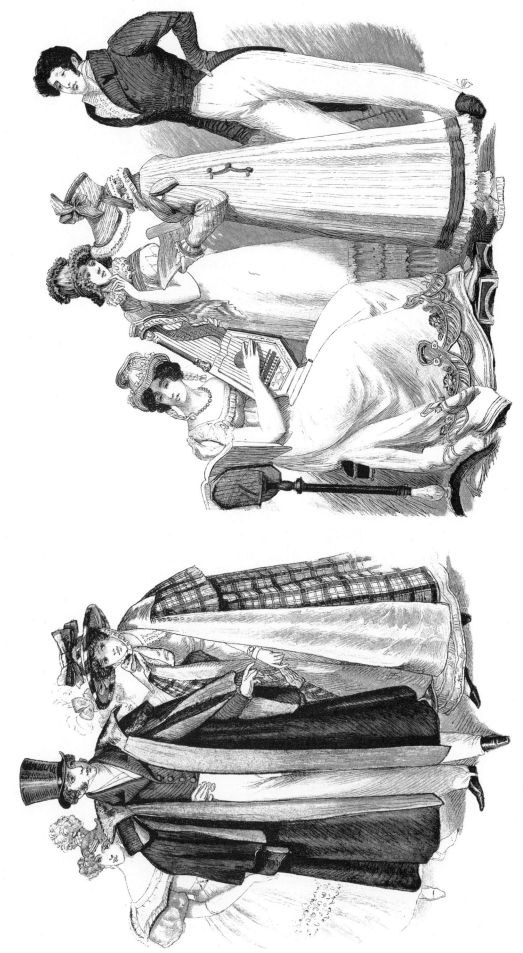

PLATE 88
FIRST HALF OF THE 19TH CENTURY; GERMANY

Upper-class dress, 1815–1820

Upper-class dress, 1825–1830

Munich, 1822:
Waitress

Middle-class
family

Upper-class dress, 1820–1825

PLATE 89

EARLY 19TH CENTURY:
BAVARIAN ARMY

Infantryman,
1814–1825

Grenadier of
the guard,
1812–1815

Light
cavalryman,
1805–1812

Cavalry captain
in the gendarmerie,
1812–1815

First lieutenant
of artillery,
1811–1825

Lieutenant
of transport,
1815–1825

Uhlan officer, 1813   Officer in the Garde du Corps, 1814–1823   Cuirassier private, 1815–1825   Trumpeter of the Garde du Corps in gala

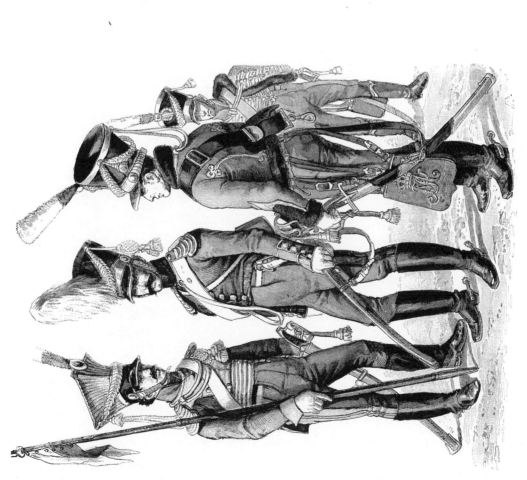

Uhlan private, 1814–1822   National light cavalryman in Prince Karl's regiment, 1813–1815   Hussar of the 2nd regiment, 1815–1822 (dissolved)

PLATE 90

LATE 19TH CENTURY;
MONASTIC ORDERS

Franciscans

Benedictines

Capuchins

Hieronymites (hermits)

PLATE 91
LATE 19TH CENTURY; ITALIAN
FOLK DRESS

In the Volscian Mountains   Fisherman from the Neapolitan Apennines

Outskirts of Rome

Genzano   Piper (*pifferario*) from the Neapolitan Apennines

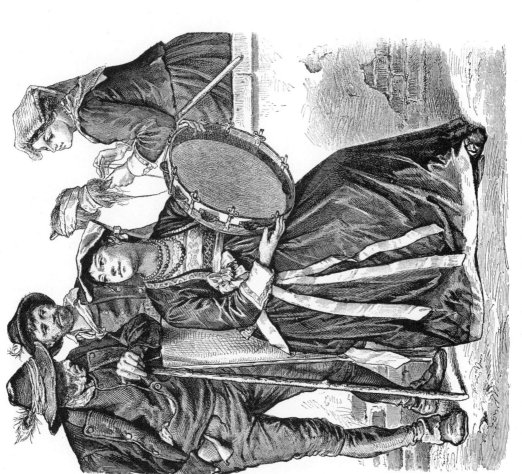

San Germano   On the Roman coast

PLATE 92

LATE 19TH CENTURY; SPANISH
FOLK DRESS

Zamora

Alicante

Granada

Valencia

Murcia

Segovia

León

PLATE 93

LATE 19TH CENTURY; DUTCH
FOLK DRESS

Frisia

Scheveningen

Marken

PLATE 94

LATE 19TH CENTURY; DUTCH
FOLK DRESS

PLATE 95

LATE 19TH CENTURY; FRENCH

FOLK DRESS (BRITTANY)

PLATE 96

LATE 19TH CENTURY; ALSATIAN
FOLK DRESS

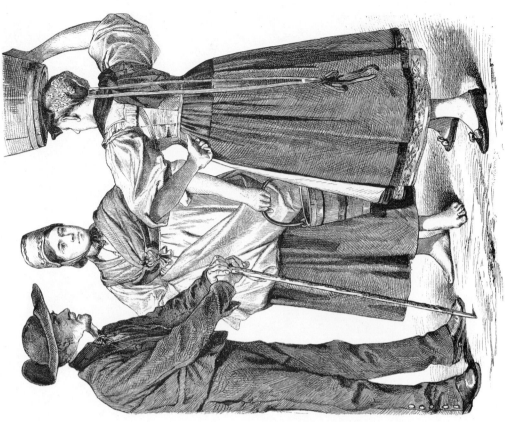

Aschbach   Weissenburg   Kochersberg

Outskirts of   Brumath   Near   Oberseebach
Schlettstadt   Weissenburg

Kochersberg   Krautgersheim   Colmar   Oberseebach
                  (Schlettstadt)

Oberseebach   Aschbach (Sulz)   Outskirts of
                           Strasbourg

PLATE 97

LATE 19TH CENTURY; SWISS FOLK DRESS

Unterwalden

Valais

Simmental

Berne

Schaffhausen

St. Gallen

Guggisberg

Zug

KNILING.

PLATE 98

LATE 19TH CENTURY; NORTH
GERMAN FOLK DRESS

Schleswig-Holstein: Peasant from   Woman from
Woman in   Hohenwested   the Halligen
Communion dress

Hamburg, man and woman   Hannover, peasant woman
from the Vierlande   from Nottendorf (Geest)

Frisian peasant women: From the island of Föhr   From Romoe   From Wyck (on Föhr)

Frisia: Girl and peasant from the Viölkaspel   Peasant woman from Ostenfeld (older costume)

PLATE 99

LATE 19TH CENTURY; GERMAN FOLK DRESS
(FORMER GRAND-DUCHY OF BADEN)

Breisgau   Witichhausen   Vilchband (Tauber area)

Hauenstein

Hardt area (Iffezheim)   Tauber area
(Witichhausen, Vilchband)

Black Forest   Schapbachthal   Hauenstein

PLATE 100

LATE 19TH CENTURY; GERMAN
FOLK DRESS (BADEN)

Guttach valley

Eastern Baar

Western Baar

Catholic Baar

Western Baar

Wedding costume, Hauenstein

PLATE 101

LATE 19TH CENTURY; GERMAN

FOLK DRESS (BADEN)

Renchthal

Hanau region

St. Georgen   Sommerau

Eastern Baar

PLATE 102

LATE 19TH CENTURY; GERMAN
FOLK DRESS (FORMER KINGDOM OF BAVARIA)

Rosenheim

Dachau

Miesbach

PLATE 103

LATE 19TH CENTURY; GERMAN

FOLK DRESS (BAVARIA)

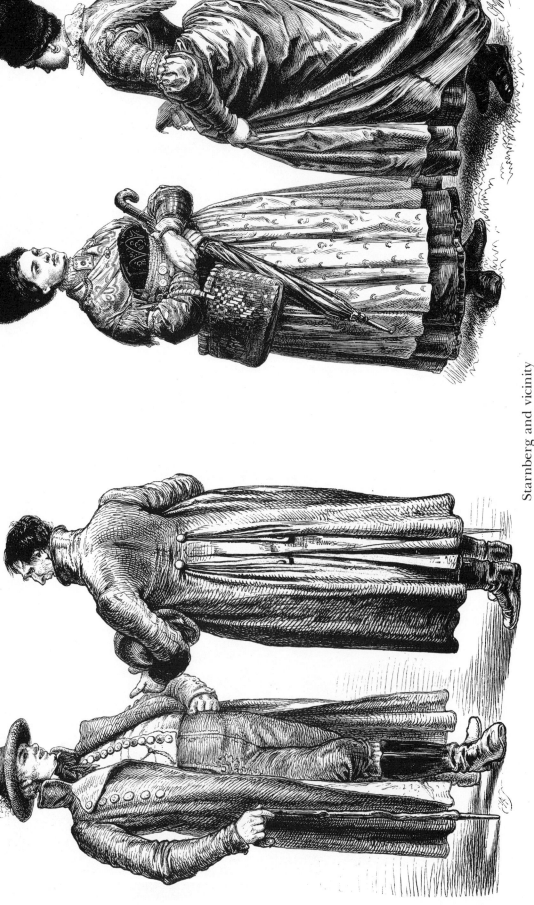

Starnberg and vicinity

Wolfratshausen

Bridesmaids, Starnberg

PLATE 104

LATE 19TH CENTURY; TYROLEAN FOLK DRESS

Grödner valley

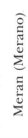

Meran (Merano)

Puster valley

Tefereggen valley

PLATE 105

LATE 19TH CENTURY; TYROLEAN
FOLK DRESS

Oetz (Adige) valley

Brixen (Bressanone)   Unterwangenberg   Brixen valley
valley

Alpbach

Wipptal

PLATE 106

LATE 19TH CENTURY; TYROLEAN
FOLK DRESS

Alt-Zillertal

Jung-Zillertal

Lower Inn valley in an earlier period

Amras—Innsbruck vicinity

PLATE 107

LATE 19TH CENTURY; DALMATIAN
FOLK DRESS

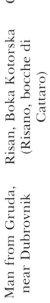

Man from Gruda, near Dubrovnik

Risan, Boka Kotorska (Risano, bocche di Cattaro)

Girl from Gruda

Inhabitants of Kruzevice (Crivoscie)

Porter from Dubrovnik (Ragusa)

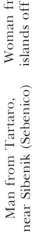

Man from Tartaro,   Woman from the   Girl from
near Sibenik (Sebenico)   islands off Sibenik   Bukovica

Girl from Draste,   Women and girl from Kruzevice,
Boka Kotorska   Boka Kotorska

PLATE 108

LATE 19TH CENTURY; FOLK DRESS
IN EUROPEAN TURKEY

(NOW PARTS OF ALBANIA, YUGOSLAVIA, BULGARIA AND GREECE)

Skodra (Scutari)   Prizren   Arnauts (Albanians) from Janina   Bulgar

Kurdish woman from Juzgat   Préveza   Chios

Monastir   Thessaly

Skodra   Adrianople (Edirne)   Saloniki

PLATE 109

LATE 19TH CENTURY; RUSSIAN
FOLK DRESS

Mordvin   Cheremiss   Estonians
(Volga Finn)   (Mari) woman

Tatars from the Crimea

Woman from Yaroslavl   Woman from Tver   Man and woman
from Kaluga

Woman from   Guberniya of   Finnish   Guberniya of
Ryazan   Voronezh   woman   Petersburg

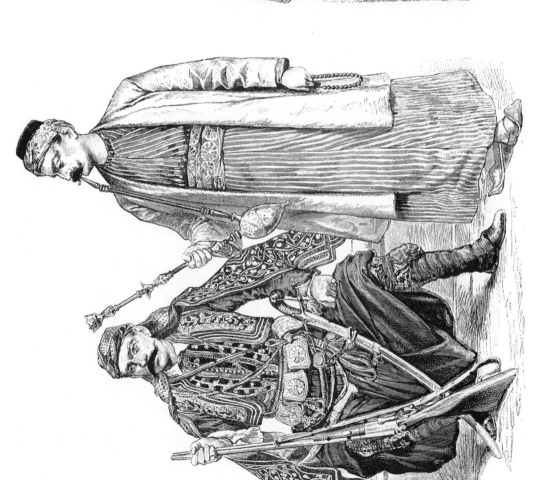

PLATE 110
LATE 19TH CENTURY; NEAR EAST

Fellah woman, vicinity of Damascus

Moslem woman, vicinity of Mecca

Vicinity of Damascus

Moslem of Damascus

Prince of Lebanon

Dervish   Syrian peasant   Young Druse   Kavass
                            woman   (police officer)
                                         in Damascus

Armenian girl   Druse   Inhabitant of
                        Damascus

PLATE 111

LATE 19TH CENTURY; EGYPT

Water seller

Inhabitants of Port Saïd

Messenger

Fruit vendor

Bedouin girl

Street dress   Slave girl   Bedouin musician

Tambourine player   Water carrier   Servant

PLATE 112
LATE 19TH CENTURY;
CAUCASUS

Cossack girl
from Cherlenaya

Woman from Akhty
in Dagestan

Woman from
Kazanistih

Bayadere from   Georgian woman   Circassian from
Shemakha   Khevsur

Cossack woman
from the Black Sea

Cossack of
the line

Inhabitant of
Kabardah

Tushin

Militiaman at Anapa   Lezghian

PLATE 113

LATE 19TH CENTURY;
CENTRAL ASIA

Dervish   Turkmen women

Man from Khiva   Emir of Bukhara   Teke Turkmen   Girl from Samarkand   Police soldier from Bukhara

Men from Khiva

Sartish women and man from Turkestan on the Chinese border

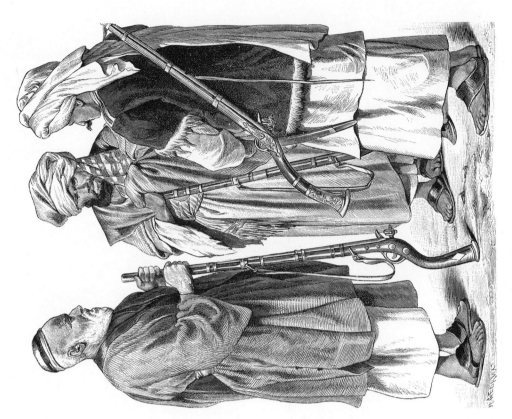

Afghans from the Khyber Pass

PLATE 114
LATE 19TH CENTURY;
AFGHANISTAN

Atah Mahomed, ambassador at Kabul, and his retinue

Afghans

(MUSEUM OF ETHNOLOGY, BERLIN)

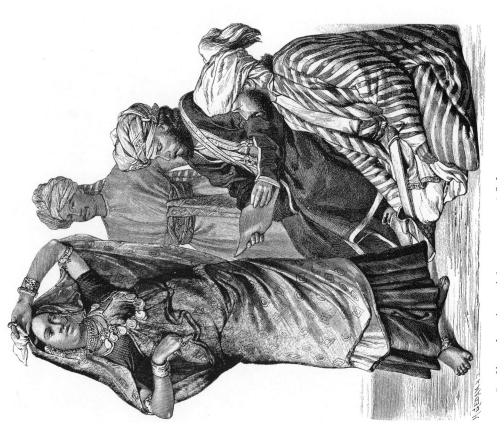

Indian dancing girl   Afghans

PLATE 115

LATE 19TH CENTURY; TIBET AND KASHMIR

Lama from Lhasa

Tibetan woman

Tibetan women and girl

Rajah

Personal guard
of the Rajah

Kashmir:
Dancing girl

Soldier of the
Maharajah

Kashmir: Men from Ladakh
in the Himalayas

PLATE 116

LATE 19TH CENTURY; INDIA
AND MALAYSIA

Klings (Telingas)

Parsees from Bombay and Singapore

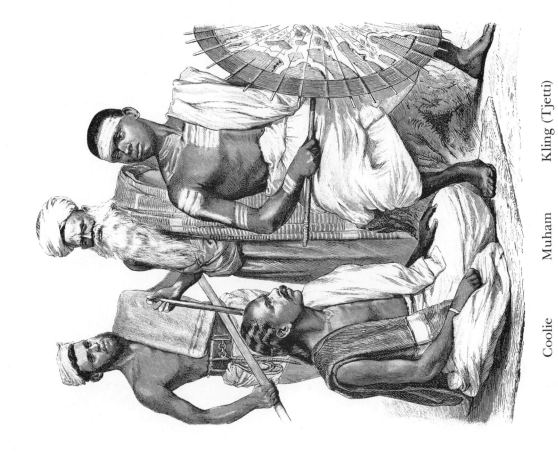

Coolie   Muham   Kling (Tjetti)

Prince and woman of Rajputana

Hindu woman

PLATE 117
LATE 19TH CENTURY
(1880); CEYLON

Singhalese

Singhalese devil dancers

Singhalese nobleman

Page of
the Governor
of Ceylon

PLATE 118

LATE 19TH CENTURY; CEYLON, JAVA, SIAM

Herald

Actors from Jaffna.

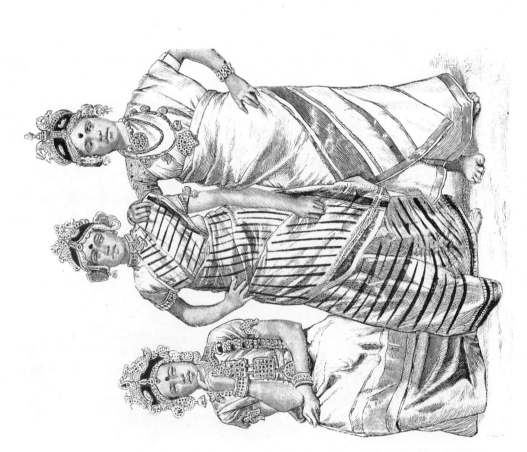

Actresses from Jaffna, on Ceylon

Actors and actresses from Siam

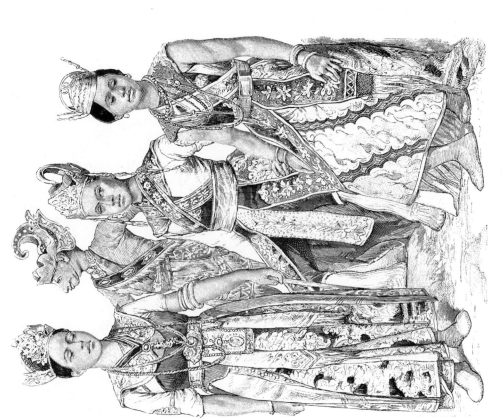

Actors and actresses from Java

PLATE 119

LATE 19TH CENTURY (1886);
SIAM AND BURMA

Burmese women

Buddhist monk   King and queen of Siam

Pu-cho weavers
from Burma

Woman from Ava,
former capital of Burma

Women of the Karen tribe (mountains of Burma)

PLATE 120

LATE 19TH CENTURY; BURMA
AND INDO-CHINA

Town dress of
woman from
Tonkin

Woman from
Tonkin

Cult
objects

Riflemen
from Tonkin

Priests from Annam

Nobleman from Annam   Girls from Annam

Burma: Officer   Minister in   Girl from   Drum
(older uniform)   gala with the   Mandalay
                   tsalve order

PLATE 121

LATE 19TH CENTURY; EAST INDIES

Regent of Cheribon, Java   Man from the island of Nias

Malays from Minangkabau, Sumatra   Bataks from Sumatra   Man from Macassar, Celebes

Princess

Dyaks

Dyaks, Borneo:
Woman

Warrior

Girl of the
aristocracy

PLATE 122

LATE 19TH CENTURY (1880);
CHINESE IN MALAYSIA

Merchant from Penang   Woman from Macao
in festive dress

Actresses

Babas from the
Straits Settlements

Shoemaker (opium eater)
from Singapore

Southern Chinese
(from Fukien)

Merchant in Penang

PLATE 123
LATE 19TH CENTURY; JAPAN

Commoners

Soldiers

Girls and women

Girl musicians   An authority

PLATE 124

LATE 19TH CENTURY; ASIATIC RUSSIA

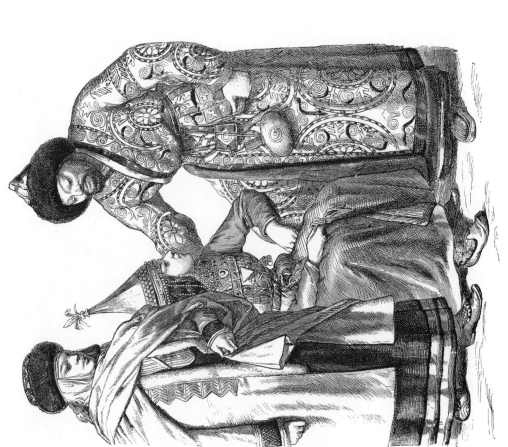

Guberniya of Tomsk   Kirghiz woman and man   Siberia Tatar woman   Kalmucks

Bashkirs   Steppe dweller   Tatar woman
from Kazan

Nomads from Amur

PLATE 125

LATE 19TH CENTURY; ASIA

Belka, Syria   Woman from
Damascus

Arab from Bagdad

Maronite from
Lebanon

Inhabitant of
Zeibek

Christian woman
from Lebanon

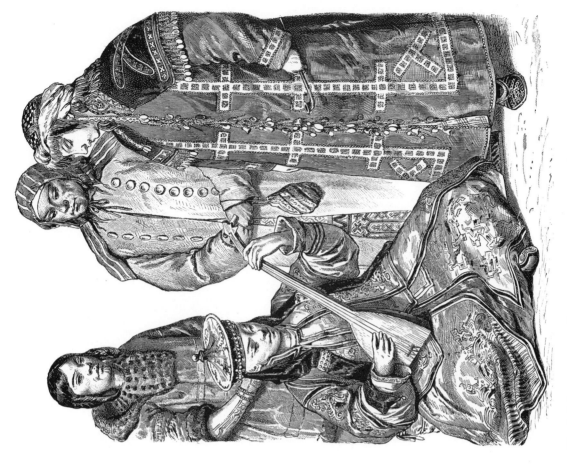

Chukchi woman   Buryat woman   Ostyaks from Obdorsk

India: King of Delhi   Brahmanic student